The Social Construction of
Black Masculinity

This book is part of the Peter Lang Political Science, Economics, and Law list.
Every volume is peer reviewed and meets
the highest quality standards for content and production.

PETER LANG
New York • Bern • Berlin
Brussels • Vienna • Oxford • Warsaw

Steven Randolph Cureton

The Social Construction of Black Masculinity

An Ethnographic Study

PETER LANG
New York • Bern • Berlin
Brussels • Vienna • Oxford • Warsaw

Library of Congress Cataloging-in-Publication Control Number: 2019008796

Bibliographic information published by **Die Deutsche Nationalbibliothek**.
Die Deutsche Nationalbibliothek lists this publication in the "Deutsche
Nationalbibliografie"; detailed bibliographic data are available
on the Internet at http://dnb.d-nb.de/.

ISBN 978-1-4331-5487-4 (hardcover)
ISBN 978-1-4331-5488-1 (ebook pdf)
ISBN 978-1-4331-5489-8 (epub)
ISBN 978-1-4331-5490-4 (mobi)
DOI 10.3726/b13348

The paper in this book meets the guidelines for permanence and durability
of the Committee on Production Guidelines for Book Longevity
of the Council of Library Resources.

This book is dedicated to Charlie Braswell.

My Father Figure, My Uncle, My Hero

Rest Easy Sir!

My God, thank you for Being Everything

So that I can be Enough.

Romans 12:3 is my Gospel Truth.

TABLE OF CONTENTS

INTRODUCTION

It Has Always Been About Race

Booker T. Washington and W. E. Burghardt Du Bois are important scholarly contributors for explaining the black experience in this country. Du Bois' perspective regarding the souls of black folk is thoroughly embedded in this book; however, Washington's Atlanta Exposition Address in 1893 has revisionist value.

> Washington stated: "Nearly sixteen millions of hands will aid you in pulling the load upward, or they will pull against you the load downward. We shall constitute one-third and more of the ignorance and crime of the South, or one-third its intelligence and progress; we shall contribute one-third to business and industrial prosperity of the South, or we shall prove a veritable body of death, stagnating, depressing, retarding every effort to advance the body politic." (Washington, 1967, p. 136)

My revision of Washington's statement reflects social changes due to the Civil Rights era. The African-American experience in contemporary America mirrors the past. There is the potential to become immersed in the American Dream. Indeed, there is that very sincere potential to be functional citizens; however, movements against the system is probable whenever there is perceived inequality and dehumanization. The post-modern black experience could be viewed as the product of institutional, systemic, cultural, and social conditions, which could yield; academics, politicians, clergymen, businessmen, doctors, lawyers, functional workers, and citizens or alternatively criminal disruptors to social continuity. Blacks have the potential to be as famous as the first black President, Barack Obama or as infamous as the so called king of the Crip gang who became a trophy kill for the state of California, Stanley "Tookie" Williams.

This Social Construction of Black Masculinity: An Ethnographic Approach examines perceptions of blacks' criminality, social regulation and control, and the nuances of negotiating manhood in troublesome environments. Stated in terms that Washington would use, I am focusing on the "veritable body of death" as a way to improve conversations about race in this country. *The Social Construction of Black Masculinity: An Ethnographic Approach* is an exercise in critical thinking concerning contextual realities and behavioral outcomes of a certain segment of black males. This book examines black masculinity using ethnography, auto-ethnography, and word audit assessments of scholars' quotes. This is an important endeavor because it seems that no matter how innocent a black man is, his presence continues to alter the normalcy of the day. Stated another way, even the most innocent and perhaps initially socially accepted black male carries the burden of a social stigma that positions him as not only troublesome, but somehow wicked.

America's social conscious seems to have not allowed degrees of freedom that affords black males the benefit of his humanity being equal to his white male counterpart. Black males' humanity continues to be judged by perceptions of his criminality. Race relations has only superficially improved, showing measured positive steps only to be eclipsed by value gap assessments relative to humanity, worthiness, and deservedness. It seems logical that periods of institutional injustice would forge the reality that blackness and criminality is a significant interactional variable in determining institutional treatment, quality of life and life course outcomes.

This book uncovers how black masculinity is vulnerable to macro and micro level social forces. It includes discussion of personal triumphs over false allegations where my teaching pedagogy was challenged as offensive. Examining the works of Du Bois is the foundation for providing some insight relative to the origins of blackness being perceived as a social hazard. The culture of policing with respect to the black community does not function independently of psychological processes operating in the minds of police officers who are attempting to serve a community that they may be alienated from and rationally fearful. Bastardized gangsterism is modern day grass roots activism and this work will attempt to provide justification for this point of view. Furthermore, the book reflects on institutional conflicts and subsequent street politics related to conducting field research on and writing about black gangs and violent subcultures. Finally, I discuss how black masculinity simultaneously loves and victimizes black women especially in those instances where relationships, and social network interactions are platforms for power struggles.

Mainstream society's apparent panic over black males as potentially dangerous whenever they are present in any social setting, inspired the focus of this book. *The Social Construction of Black Masculinity: An Ethnographic Approach* details how black males negotiate manhood in socially disorganized, resource strain communities that are beset by a subculture of violence and the prevalence of gangs. According to 2014 census data, black working-to-middle class incomes 35,000 to 100,000 were 65% compared to black household incomes 15,000 and under (22%). In spite of the majority of households falling in the working-to-middle class, or upper class (over 100,000 at 13%), the narrative that black masculinity is problematic, troublesome, deserving of incarceration, and even lethal policing reflects an over investment in the notion that black masculinity is synonymous with elevated criminality.

There is no doubt that this notion is partly influenced by the subcultural practices, criminogenic pursuits, family dysfunction and disproportionately incarcerated individuals that are most likely residents of those households that earn up to 15,000. It seems that the African-American permanent underclass or household incomes at 15,000 or less has a larger negative impact on society's collective conscience. It seems that negative stigmas associated with the permanent underclass over-ride positive images that should be derived from the fact that the majority working, middle and upper class African-American households are more likely routinely engaged in conventional citizenship. Additionally, there seems to be too much emphasis on the disproportionate representation of African-Americans that are incarcerated. African-American males and females are approaching 1 million of the 2.3 million total incarcerated individuals in America. There appears to be a degree of dismissiveness regarding the fact that approximately 41 million African-Americans are not incarcerated. In spite of these overwhelming numbers representing conformity, the prevailing narrative about African-Americans, particularly African-American males is that they are dangerous because of predispositions to be criminal (Glaude, 2016; Welch, 2007; Wilson, 2009).

Chapter 1, *Scholarly Fingerprint: A Research Note* provides a summary of my scholarship. My research offers a legitimate sociological inquiry concerning the nature of black masculinity within the context of criminogenic, deviant and violent environments. This is important given that mainstream society's collective conscience about black manhood appears to concentrate on those residing in the permanent underclass more than working, middle and upper classes. Moreover, black masculinity is stigmatized given excessive and almost exclusive concentration on black males residing in permanent underclass environments.

Chapter 2, *I Will Dig a Ditch, Just Give Me My Good Name Back* represents full disclosure regarding a personal ordeal. On September 25, 2013, I was informed that I was being accused by two white female students of sexual harassment and racial discrimination. With the start of a Title IX investigation underway, my character was officially under attack. My initial feelings were of confusion and despair, imagining that my innocence did not stand a chance against allegations coming from two white female students on a predominantly white campus. I just knew this would be a case of being menaced by race. Meaning being black would be enough to tarnish my career by finding me guilty of sexual harassment and racial discrimination. The investigation represented a process that pushed me to the brink of pedagogic uncertainty and suicidal thoughts.

Chapter 3, *Du Bois' Souls of Black and White Folk: Can't Out Run Caste in America* explores the nuances of society's collective conscience with respect to the souls of black and white folks. According to Du Bois there is a veil whereby soul estimations serve as concrete messages guiding blacks' life course outcomes. Are race relations contingent upon assumptions that blacks are the antithesis of whites and that black criminality negates the potential to be equally human?

Chapter 4, *Policing Black Bodies: Lethal Predatory Habits*, examines cultural codes that appear to dictate policing out of fear, heightened oppressive tactics, exaggerated oppression and ultimately use of lethal force. The question is, does the culture of policing lower reverence of life when it comes to black people? Chapter 4, explores plausible explanations that are worthy of consideration.

Chapter 5, *Protest Spirit: Bastardized Activism in Gangsterism*, re-examines information offered in, *Hoover Crips: When Cripin' Becomes a Way of Life and Black Vanguards and Black Gangsters: From Seeds of Discontent to a Declaration of War*. The primary goal of this chapter is to not only provide a brief synopsis of both books but to place them within the context of modern day black gangsterism and social activist's movements. A final charge of this chapter is to address the question; are black gangs capable of returning to activist's roots?

Chapter 6, *Edge Research: Taking in Ganglands and Violent Scenes*, examines the dangers associated with doing participant observation research on gangs and the subculture of deviance, crime and violence happening in nightclubs. Black researchers have an obligation to disclose social truths about subcultural codes and have to also balance the ethics associated with observing deviant, criminal and violent subcultures.

Chapter 7, *Hulking Out: White Males' Response to Bullying, Humiliation, Rejection, Intimidation, and Perceived Injustice in an Academic Setting*, represents an important discussion given what appears to be an increasing tide involving engaging in mass murder to validate social legitimacy and perceived personal entitlements. With what seems to be a perpetual demonstration of mass murder, particularly in locales considered soft targets, this is a timely book chapter that should be reprinted. Hence, this represents a bonus chapter that I authored and has already appeared in Gause's (2017) *Leadership, Equity, and Social Justice in American Higher Education*. The relevancy of the chapter on mass murder for this book is the discussion regarding differential racial socialization, which seems significantly related to targeted murder for blacks and mass murder for whites.

Chapter 8, *A Love of Our Own: The Manner in Which Black Men Love*, examines Eldridge Cleaver's assessment of a black mitosis and an assessment of the troubled love tradition between black males and females as frameworks to understand intra-racial relationships. Cleaver is a highly controversial figure who proclaimed hate for black women, raped black girls, and had an instinctive attraction to white women. He evolved professing a born again spirit that positioned black women as deserving of a black man's love. It is ironic that I circle back to discuss *Soul on Ice* given this book was the source of tension that generated a Title IX investigation.

Chapter 9, *Closure Is All I Need to Get By*, represents a summary of the book, acknowledges the important contributions of others who have inspired the writing of this book. Additionally, this chapter is simply an exercise in exhaling after the end of an emotionally invested endeavor.

A primary assumption of this book is black-to-white race relations is significantly related to perceptions of black manhood and their seemingly over indulgence in crime. What's more their proportional participation in crime and incarceration leads to moral panic regarding their potential to be criminal more than their law abiding behavior. Black masculinity is defined as being independently responsible for a dignified existence. Whereby black men act to obtain the adoration of their companions, black women, and the recognition of respectable fatherhood from their children. The focus is on the behavioral outcomes of black men who set out to seize upon their version of black masculinity within socially disorganized, resource strained, embattled communities. Residency in these communities causes masculinity to be differentially experienced because of varying degrees of deprivation and marginalization. Therefore, a more appropriate discourse about black masculinity should be contextually specific in order to prohibit treating it as an intra-race neutral concept. The ultimate hope is to generate discussions that lead to actions that improve race relations between blacks and whites in America.

· 1 ·

SCHOLARLY IDENTITY

A Research Note

The purpose of this chapter is to familiarize the reader with my research interests in an effort to lay the foundation for this book being a logical extension of my sociological research on black masculinity. The initial stage of my research (1999–2004) was more reflective of mainstream sociology and criminology. My research, mostly quantitative, did not deviate from examining well established theories with respect to racial declination and life course outcomes. As a sociologist, I am interested in whether race significantly affects blacks' life chances. William Julius Wilson's (1978) book *The Declining Significance of Race* suggests that changes in the American economy and social structure effected changes in life course opportunities, social mobility and social capital. According to Wilson (1978), class position more than minority group affiliation is significantly related to social, economic, educational, and cultural success. Alternatively, E. Franklin Frazier's perspective on the black bourgeoisie implies that minority status continues to significantly impact social, economic, educational, and cultural success. Cureton (2002) *An Assessment of Wilson and Frazier's Perspectives on Race and Racial Life Chances, African-American Perspectives*, examined the legitimacy of both perspectives, using data from the National Football League (NFL) and National Basketball Association (NBA). The prevailing conclusion was that white governance over opportunity structures has not significantly changed enough to suggest that class position more than race is more important in predicting social mobility.

Additionally, I was interested in race and academic performance. Sociologically, my research examined how African-Americans' social experiences impact academic pursuits on predominantly white campuses. Given educational success is a key ingredient for African-Americans' quality of life, it seems important to examine the determinants of academic success. Cureton (2003) *Race Specific College Student Experiences on a Predominantly White Campus, The Journal of Black Studies,* examined black and white students' experiences with adverse situations un-related to college, perceptions of the college environment, perceptions of self, and perceptions of campus police officers. The most interesting finding is that adverse situations are not racially exclusive given white and black students have experienced similar situational circumstances.

As a criminologist, my research focused on the nature of social order and social regulation. The critical issue that my research addressed was whether blacks are being afforded equitable liberty, free of prejudice and partial justice or are blacks being subjected to a criminal justice system where justice is dependent upon social, economic, and cultural characteristics? Consensus theory posits that the disproportionately higher number of blacks (compared to whites) being processed through the legal system is the result of justifiable sanctions. Alternatively, conflict theory contends that blacks' higher rates of legal attention are significantly related to discretionary practices. Cureton (2001) *An Empirical Test of the Social Threat Phenomenon: Using 1990 Census and Uniform Crime Reports, Journal of Criminal Justice;* Cureton (2000) *Justifiable Arrests or Discretionary Justice: Predictors of Racial Arrest Differentials, Journal of Black Studies;* Cureton (1999) *Differential Black/White Arrest Rates: Offending Behavior or Discretionary Justice, African-American Research Perspectives;* and Cureton (2000) *Determinants of Black/White Arrest Differential: A Review of the Literature* in Markowitz and Brown's (eds.), *The System in Black and White: Exploring the Connections Between Race, Crime and Justice,* represents three research articles and one book chapter that addressed the predictors of black/white arrest differentials. The findings in no way settle the debate concerning the nature of discretionary justice; however, the empirical evidence does suggest that the criminal justice system may have been relatively partial and impartial relative to its sanctioning of blacks. Thus, when it comes to equitable justice, there should be a measure of caution when proclaiming the possibility that discrimination exists.

After reading the literature on the African-American gang phenomenon and interacting with black gang members for well over a decade, I strongly believe that the black gang phenomenon is a seriously misunderstood issue. Thus the second stage (2005 to present) of my research concerns black masculinity within the context of a subculture of violence and ganglands. There were theorists (e.g., Anderson, Katz and Frazier), cultural scholars (e.g., Du Bois, Wilson, West, and Dyson) and thoroughly immersed gangsters (e.g., Stanley "Tookie" Williams, and Sanyika Shakur, better known as Monster Kody) that provided a blueprint to examine black gangsterism. Jack Katz's (1988) *Seductions of Crime: Moral and Sensual Attractions to Doing Evil* offers a street elite perspective that males seek the gang as a way of transcending the negative emotions they experience as a result of perceived societal rejection. Katz's coverage of street elite formations as the result of economic, social and cultural forces moving against groups of people and those very same people embracing an aura, energy and spirit of rebellion, encouraged me to not turn a blind eye to the energetic aura or notions of emotional gravitation that significantly impact gang formations and individual's decision to join an already established gang. E. Franklin Frazier (1968) *E. Franklin Frazier on Race Relations* asserted that a significant proportion of black intellectuals have done very little to advance proper understanding of the black experience in America. Specifically, Frazier's call to action was for black intellectuals to examine the adverse impact that relative integration and assimilation has had on black people. Frazier inspired me to begin researching black gangsterism from the perspective of residents who were negatively impacted by black flight.

Sociology and a more concentrated subfield of mainstream criminology, African-American criminology can be used to objectively present the "soul" of a people because sociology and African-American criminology's greatest commodity is its cause/effect explanatory framework, which promotes humanistic understanding. In combination, sociology and African-American criminology lead me to gravitate towards ethnography to examine the impact of the race variable on black gangsterism. In May of 1999, I conducted a three year field research project that initially started in Greensboro, North Carolina but quickly pivoted to the gang capital of America, South Central, Los Angeles. The result of this ethnographic research is Cureton (2002) *Introducing Hoover: I'll Ride for You Gangsta* in Huff's (ed.), *Gangs in America III* and Cureton (2008) *Hoover Crips: When Cripin' Becomes a Way of Life.* The research objective was to provide authentic truisms concerning the origins, refuge, salvation, life and death consequences, spirituality, and pursuit of manhood in communities that are ganglands.

The second stage of my research is best captured by stating that I examined how black masculinity is negotiated within the context of deviant subcultures, violence and gangsterism? My research demonstrates a love for the richness of qualitative data, which led to going to South Central, Los Angeles to research and produce a book on the Hoover Crips, followed by a sixteen year exploration of the subculture of violence by way of being a participant observant as a body guard to musical rappers, and professional athletes as well as a bouncer in clubs that are known for attracting drug dealers and residents of communities that experience violence on a routine basis. With respect to researching black masculinity, I concentrated on residents who could be classified as the permanent underclass. William Julius Wilson's work on the permanent underclass and his (2009) book *More than Just Race: Being Black and Poor in the Inner City* provided more encouragement for me to continue to explore the complexities of cultural forces on black manhood. Elijah Anderson's (1999) *Code of the Street: Decency, Violence, and the Moral Life of the Inner City*, Stanley "Tookie" Williams' (2009) *Blue Rage Black Redemption*, and Sanyika Shakur's (1993) autobiographical book *Monster: The Autobiography of an L.A. Gang Member* focused my energy on black males' pursuit of respectable manhood while confined to residency in troublesome environments.

The following is a chronological synopsis of my scholarship leading up to *The Social Construction of Black Masculinity: An Ethnographic Study*. The first article is Cureton and Bellamy's (2007) *Gangster "Blood" Over College Aspirations: The Implications of Gang Membership for One Black Male College Student*, *Journal of Gang Research*.

Rochelle Bellamy was recruited from my undergraduate class, Contemporary Gangs in America (Sociology 425 writing intensive). A mini grant was awarded by the University of North Carolina at Greensboro's undergraduate research assistantship program. Working with Rochelle represented a collaborative commitment to conduct research with undergraduate students. Rochelle's contribution was that she assisted with the review of literature and transcribed the interview with gang member Sweet T. The Contemporary Gangs in America course waived pre-requisite requirements for gang members enrolled in college. Sweet T, volunteered to be interviewed out of jealousy. Sweet T, admitted that he felt angry that the course seemed to devote more time to rival Crip gangs. He wanted more coverage of Blood Gangs. Sweet T, suggested that his story was unique in that he was still an active member of the Rigsby Court Gangster Bloods out of San Antonio, Texas and that he was on track to graduate from college. He added that being in college, in no way negated his gang ties and that he was committed to the routine activities of gangsterism. Unfortunately, Sweet T, dropped out of school, fifteen credits shy of earning a degree due to being required to handle gang related issues in San Antonio. In other words, Sweet T, was called upon as the gang demanded that he return to deal with the death of a gang member.

The significant contribution of Cureton and Bellamy's work is that it represented a single case analysis, which highlighted the fact that gangs could be organized enough to exert social pressures on members in a manner that interferes with conventional activity. This finding contributes to the growing body of literature concerning the presence of gangs on college campuses and the influence of gang membership for those individuals who remain committed enough to yield to the demands of gangsterism.

The second research production during the second research stage is my book (2008), *Hoover Crips: When Cripin' Becomes a Way of Life*. In my opinion, one of the many reasons Anderson's (1999), *Code of the Street: Decency, Violence, and the Moral Life of the Inner City*, is considered an ethnographic classic is that it challenged long standing narratives that a certain segment of the black population embraced violence as a primary means to settle conflict due to pathologies, and violent predispositions. Arguably, the nature of black criminality remains situated in narratives related to innate predisposition by nature of race, and pathology steeped in depravity. Anderson's walk down Germantown, revealed that there is a continuum where civility and drifts towards violence is contingent upon situational circumstances that present challenges to respect. One takeaway from Anderson's work is that residency in lower strata neighborhoods does not automatically guarantee embracing and participating in violence, rather residents' routine activities present encounters that are immediately processed as situations deserving of decency, civility or perhaps violence. Engaging in violence is precipitated by situational ethics related to negotiating social capital relative to respect. Behavioral outcomes that counter challenges to perceived assaults on one's character or affronts to respect are the result of subcultural codes or a set of normative expectations. Social currency is extremely important to intra-residential social status and peer interactions.

In similar fashion, I wanted to walk down Hoover, a gang dominated neighborhood in South Central, Los Angeles. I was curious as to how Anderson's code of the street would apply to just one neighborhood in the gang capital of America. In other words, was respect just as important for black males in an area where gangs are thoroughly entrenched in the social fabric of a neighborhood?

Entering the field, a ground zero neighborhood, the likes of Hoover provided the opportunity to witness the nuances of negotiating manhood in a gangland during a time when neighborhoods were engaged in gang wars. The research project covered 24 days, (almost evenly split between two summers in 1999 and 2000). Stated another way, my field work totaled 170 hours, including observations and interactions, where 12 original gangsters were interviewed (only 8 actually recorded), 25 peer cohort groups ranging in ages 14 to 35 were interacted with via focus groups while walking through the Hoover neighborhood. Another 50 people were observed, and had field notes written about them, for a total of 87, community members, gang affiliated, associated, or thoroughly immersed gang bangers. Hoover consists of 9 streets or branches from 43rd to 52nd, to 59th, to 74th, to 83rd, to 92nd, to 94th, to 107th, and finally 112th street. The emergence of black gangs has been relegated to a late 60's to early 70's phenomenon that involved subcultural/gang formations fueled by criminogenic opportunities associated with the gun and drug underground economy. At worst black gangs have been described as pathological adaptations to the organized confusion associated with ghetto/urbanity, and at best black gangs have been elevated to uncivil predatory groups programmed to inflict social and physical devastation. The ethnographic approach produced some findings that should be explored in the future: (1) gang membership both causes criminal behavior and attracts boys who are already doing crime; (2) gangs attract already delinquent individuals who once a member, are affiliated with a group that encourages further criminogenic behaviors; (3) ghetto confined boys act on an agenda to become ghetto superstars in the hood; (4) becoming a ghetto superstar requires actively pursuing and protecting territory ("the greens") which are part of establishing a gang banger's identity ("the game"); and (5) central to "the greens" and "the game" is a group of already established aggressive men, who provide an avenue for young boys to reach their goal of ghetto superstardom. The fresh element here is that gang recruitment seems obsolete. Moreover, in an economic and resource strained, isolated environment, the refuge offered by Hoover is fundamentally essential to black males' righteous survival. The gang is a product of the farmer's harvest. Meaning the gang is a manifestation of social, political, economic, structural, cultural and spiritual shifts in the black community. This means that the gang is a social construction and a product of life course experiences. More specifically, Cureton's Emergent Gangsterism Perspective (EGP, 1920–2009 and beyond) suggests that the context of gangsterism is defined community, community conversion, gangster colonization, and gangster politicization. The EGP perspective suggests that blacks have a unique history of generational humanistic deprivation that has contributed to the decline of the black community and the formation of black gangs. The implications suggest that solutions to the gang phenomenon should focus on social, political, economic, structural, cultural and spiritual deficits. The fear of punishment ingredient inherent in the criminal justice system is based on the rational that choices are made based on a cost/ benefit analysis, yet the cost/benefit analysis is subject to residency in a gangland, an intense counter subculture operating outside of conventionalism. In other words, the germ for gangsterism is airborne, independent of people but very dependent upon the pursuit of respectable living. Hence, we can warehouse the problem by imposing severe sanctions but incarceration is just postponing regeneration.

The impact of the Hoover research is: (1) it provided an updated, version of Chicago style field research on black gangsterism; (2) Cureton's Emergent Gangsterism Perspective (EGP) was introduced as a black gang formation perspective; and (3) the impact of racial and social currency of the researcher was discussed as a contributing social artifact to research on a black gang in a black community. Ethnographic research on black street gangs, particularly black street gangs the likes of the Hoover Crips is scarce. The result is less than accurate explanations about black gangs continue to garner attention instead of timely perspectives regarding why black gangs continue to thrive in permanent underclass black communities.

The next two articles and book are based on the following assumptions: (1) black flight had a negative impact effecting a permanent underclass whose residents, specifically male formed and participated in predatory gangs; (2) gangs represent the most dominant socialization institution in communities beset by social disorganization; and (3) the gang is the gateway, cultural filter and vessel for negotiating black manhood. Cureton (2009) *Something Wicked This Way Comes: A Historical Account of Black Gangsterism Offers Wisdom and Warning for African-American Leadership, Journal of Black Studies* is an article designed to provide a brief history about black street and prison gangs. The significant contribution of this research article rests with its declaration that black gangs are the most powerful socialization agent within certain black communities.

The gang has consistently been a socialization agent influencing how black males navigate their social world specifically in cities that have a significant representation of gangs to be classified as ganglands. Black gangs have a long legacy that includes community development, activism, informal social regulation and control of intra-community violence. However, the civility of black gangs receives little attention because it does not quite align with mainstream society's collective moral panic relative to black male criminality. Hence, the primary focus on black gangs has centered on its criminogenic nature.

It remains a social fact that the legacy of black gangsterism reveals that black gangs were civil enough to assist in the struggle for equality. Some black gangs were endorsed as positive community organizations by local political leadership (i.e., Crips, Vice Lords, and Disciples), whereas others secured government grants and purchased buildings that were central locations for community improvement programs (i.e., Vice Lords, P-Stones/El Rukns). Alternatively, history reveals that regardless of positive intentions, black street gangs altered their course of action aligning themselves with criminogenic opportunities due partly to federal, state, and local governments' legitimate and illegitimate practices, the criminal justice machine's discretionary justice, and urban criminogenic vices (i.e., hustling, gambling, running numbers, pimping, prostitution, and drugs).

> If only black leadership had assisted these gangs when they were sparring with the federal government and corrupt police practices, perhaps some direction, resources, and social networking could have changed the course of the gang. On the contrary, black leadership and the black middle class abandoned the urban poor, and as more and more older males were shipped to the modern-day slave ships (prisons), the community was left to the youth who developed a "lord of the flies" mentality. (Cureton, 2009, pp. 349–350)

Cureton (2010) Lost Souls of Society Become Hypnotized by Gangsterism, *Journal of Gang Research* was inspired by Jim Brown and E. Franklin Frazier's similar contention that devastating outcomes to the black community resulted from marginalization and intra-racial class alienation. Jim Brown in particular opined that gangs represent the most troublesome and burdensome element facing the black community. The article details social force and social conflict correlates of black gangsterism. Moreover, in the spirit of Stanley "Tookie" Williams' (2009) peace treaty accord, I discuss the need for a black youth liberation movement.

The crux of the black youth liberation movement discussed in this article is assuming accountability for the problems related to gangsterism including the lethal predation linked to gang banging in the black community.

The ultimate goal of Cureton's (2011). *Black Vanguards and Black Gangsters: From Seeds of Discontent to a Declaration of War* is to explore the historical and contemporary realities of black gangsterism in America using the legacy of race as the starting point of analysis. The challenge for the African-American male in America has been a constant struggle to reconcile the seemingly dominant social dynamic that black masculinity is significantly less human than white masculinity. This book examined black males' behavioral manifestations within the context of a perceived war against his humanity and a more concentrated battle against like circumstanced males residing in communities in close proximity. The evidence suggests that is probable that these men will invest in any rebellious group, especially if that group provides opportunities for lifestyle improvements and respect.

> It does not matter how these groups are perceived in mainstream America because these marginalized black men are operating in accordance to their immediate subculture. Hence, it should be no surprise when marginalized black men decide to obey whatever, normative expectation, and/or associate with whatever group that seems to offer personal validation. (Cureton, 2011, pp. 2–3)

The next two journal articles examined the influence of socialization and peer group social audiences on black masculinity. The expanded lens is that black masculinity was examined in environments, not necessarily dominated by gangs but still had an element of being exposed to violence. Failing to fully divest myself from the ethnographic excitement that the Hoover gang research provided, I embarked upon another ethnographic project, closer to home where I could be exposed to the environment on a routine basis. Understanding the importance of social capital gleaned from my research on the Hoover gang, I continued researching the subculture of violence but this time as a participant observant. Cureton (2011), *Night-Crawlers: The Potential Health Risks Associated with Criminogenic Masculinity and Clubbing* was a product of a ten year period of being a bouncer/body guard. As a bouncer/body guard I was positioned as safety personnel, responsible for deterring and suppressing arguments and violence occurring in nightclubs. The fundamental takeaway from this article is that going out to night clubs for leisurely fun can turn out to be a health risk depending on the population of club patrons that the night club attracts.

Cureton and Wilson's (2012) *The Deceptive Black Knight Campaign: Clique Loyalty and Sexual Conquest, Journal of Black Masculinity* examined the social framework of black males with respect to engaging in behaviors that affirmed masculinity in the eyes of their peers, while simultaneously attempting to negotiate a successful mating game that unfortunately has very little to do with being in a monogamous relationship and even less to do with fatherhood. Dr. Wilson co-authored and wrote the research field note concerning middle-school females' role as not being "passive and clueless about the sexual promiscuity of the boys they choose to interact and engage in some form of relationship" (Cureton and Wilson, 2012, pp. 16–17).

Fundamentally, the research attempted to disentangle the social issues relative to masculinity in socially disorganized communities. Moreover, Cureton's Deceptive Black Knight Campaign (DBKC) a framework that integrated Anderson's code of the street and mating game and Sykes and Matza's neutralization theory was introduced. The prevailing narrative is that clique loyalties dominate black males' social construction of reality, which includes criminogenic participation and subscribing to objectification and sexual exploitation of young females. The impact of this article is that it contributes to Anderson's perspective on the dating and mating game. The Deceptive Black Knight Campaign explores male cohort loyalties and relationship pursuits. A very surface level speculation on feminism, reveals that cultural proscriptions coupled with dysfunctional and irresponsible black masculinity combined to victimize black females.

More recently, there has been a social panic over mass shootings occurring on school grounds and the murderous campaign that has made Chicago's Chiraq infamous. Listening to media accounts about mass shooting, default to scapegoating, where mental illness is blamed for mass shootings more than a reasoning criminal mind that strategically planned a killing campaign, inspired a book chapter on mass shootings. Additionally, the murder rate for Chicago's south-side communities continues to receive considerable media attention to the point where south-side predominantly black communities adopted the assumptions that their murder rate rivals that of killings happening during the Iraq War. Seemingly this social proclamation has become a badge of honor and certainly begs explanation so that we don't again become hostage to the narrative of pathological violence over the impact of adverse social and cultural forces. Cureton's (2017) *Hulking Out: White Males' Response to Bullying, Humiliation, Rejection, Isolation, and Perceived Injustice in an Academic Setting*, in Gause (ed.), *Leadership, Equity, and Social Justice in Amer-*

ican Higher Education: A Reader appears in this book as a reprint. This chapter clearly identifies white males more than black males as triggermen in mass shootings on school grounds. Moreover, this chapter dispels the narrative that mass shooters are more mentally ill than rational calculating murderers. Additionally, I contend that white privilege emboldens white males to engage in perceived vigilantism, righteous slaughters and/or symbolic murder, while black males are conditioned to engage in targeted lethal predation given they subscribe to codes of the street and therefore are more likely to settle disputes off of school grounds.

The significance of Cureton's (2017) article *Chiraq: Oppression, Homicide, Concentrated Misery and Gangsterism in Chicago, Journal of Gang Research,* is that the narrative of killing campaigns happening for no reason is challenged. In fact, killing campaigns in Chiraq are the result of long standing housing maneuvers, segregation, and differential treatment of white gangs compared to black gangs, intra-racial rival gang proximity issues (e.g., bunching rival gangs in residential locales where they are forced to see one another on a daily basis) coupled with gang fragmentation without hierarchical leadership.

The future is now for examining black masculinity as having a dual effect of victimizing and being made to be victims. The following projects represent research that is ethnographic and auto-ethnographic. Both projects are opportunities to take stock in the type of research and methods of inquiry that I have used to examine black masculinity as a social construction.

Ransaw and Gause, recruited me to collaborate as a section editor for their book, *Handbook of Research on Black Males.* My job was to recruit four contributors for a section on black masculinity and social justice. Dr. Simpkins'(2019) chapter *Victimized, Victim: The Consciousness of Black Femininity in the Image of Masculinity* contributed a feminist's perspective on how black masculine frameworks when used by black females to judge other black females in social and professional settings, effect female-to-female victimization, either by character assassinations and violence while growing up and professional bullying within the work place. Dr. Dennis' (2019) chapter, *Black male suicide: Inward expressed frustration and aggression,* detailed how differences in coping strategies for black males could lead to inward aggression and ultimately suicide. According to Dr. Dennis, black males experience pressure, frustration and inward aggression when dealing with failures and insecurities particularly in places where there are noticeable differences in racial social status and perceived social mobility. Dr. Collins' (2019) chapter, *The Media Assault on the Black Male: Echoes of Public Lynching and Killing the Modern*

Terror of Jack Johnson, examined how there continues to be an onslaught of character assassinations with respect to black masculinity in cinema. Dr. Monell's (2019) chapter, *A Preliminary Examination of Hegemonic Masculinity: Definitional Transference of Black Masculinity Effecting Lethal Tactics against Black Males*, discussed the psychological definitions operating in the minds of law enforcement agents, when encountering and deciding to use lethal force on black males. Taken together, this section examines the impact of social injustice on black manhood, and how black masculinity is perceived as volatile enough to warrant lethal force. Moreover, this section explores the level of intra-racial social injustice and its impact on intra-racial victimization.

For a total of seventeen years my research involved field research on one of the largest African-American street gangs in South Central, the Hoovers, and I have actively participated in Greensboro North Carolina's night life scene as club security at places that cater to gangsters, hustlers, and drug dealers. Both environments similarly revealed that masculine performances involved negotiating a respectable reputation, which is contingent upon obeying criminogenic and violent street code ethics. Hoovers allowed me to explore through observation the nuances of gangsterism. Alternatively, exploring the realities of Greensboro's underbelly nightclubs involved participation with respect to controlling violence. It is true that being an African-American male served as a critical ingredient affecting my drift from an outsider to insider for both research projects on Hoover and Greensboro's night-life scene. It is equally true that once on the inside, there was no clear path out. I have divested enough to provide objective reflection and yet I acknowledge that I am not completely divorced given connections and ongoing relationships with gang members, party promoters, former bouncers, and patrons who continue to recognize me.

The purpose of observing Hoovers in South Central, Los Angeles and becoming a bouncer for several violent clubs was to decode behaviors related to gangsterism and the subculture of violence and to identify value systems (gangster and street code ethics) that black males endorse as evidence of masculinity. It's been 17 years (dating back to 1999) of ethnographic research on the Hoover Gang and Greensboro's nightlife subculture of violence. The participant observant balance has led to interesting self-discovery. Whether I was observing Hoovers (1999–2000) or participating in regulating violence at night clubs, (2001–2016) my reservations approached concern about the possibility that this method of research could eventually lead to personal injury and even a casualty of lethal violence. I managed to repress my concern by trusting what I thought was a calling to understand black masculinity, violence and gangs.

The important contribution of my book chapter, *Hoovers and Night Crawlers: When Outside In Becomes Inside Out (2019)*, in Ransaw and Gause (eds.) *Handbook of Research on Black Males*, is that it dealt with three critical issues black researchers conducting field research on deviant communities contend with: (1) maintaining an appropriate distance in order to be objective; (2) contemplating withholding social facts out of fear that information could further stigmatize and/or demonstrate racial depravity; and (3) assuming that racial allegiance endows the researcher with racial expertise. These race specific issues were countered by maintaining a social scientific lens grounded by two logical perspectives, street elites and code of the street, respectively. Moreover, the hesitancy to withhold social facts was eased by an obligation to remain as objective as possible while also being sensitive to the reality that racial life course outcomes are significantly related to institutional opportunity access, economic, social, cultural, residency, and spiritual variables.

The overall impact of my research has been to provide legitimate sociological inquiry and analysis of how black males negotiate their manhood in troublesome environments. This is important given that mainstream society's collective conscience about black manhood appears to concentrate on those residing in the permanent underclass. To this end, negative racial casting of black masculinity seems beholden to the permanent black underclass more than working, middle and upper classes. This book will move the social narrative about black males from one of predisposed criminality and pathology to social adaptations to community dysfunction.

· 2 ·

I WILL DIG A DITCH,
JUST GIVE ME MY GOOD NAME BACK

I have decided to disclose a personal ordeal because it represented an example of being menaced by race by way of an attempted character assassination. Moreover, I prefer to own it as part of my black experience. On July 19, 2017 about three years and 10 months after two white female students accused me of sexual harassment and racial discrimination, I stepped back into Graham 203, the classroom where I had taught Sociology 364, an undergraduate course on African-American Social Thought. For almost four years I had avoided making eye contact and going near that room. I was initially, hesitant to touch the door knob because behind that door something horrible transpired. I will not claim independent bravery, I was accompanied by a friend. Upon entering the classroom my eyes fixated on the two chairs my accusers had sparingly occupied. I walked off the distance from those seats to the teaching podium, which was approximately twenty five feet. How could these students who sat in a room with twenty one other students, twenty five feet away come away with such devastating accusations? The complaint was that my lectures made them feel sexually uncomfortable, and that I had discriminated against them by referring to them as white girls.

During a face-to-face interview with the Deputy Investigator and Investigator (a committee of two), one of the Investigators suggested seeking counseling given the range of emotions that I openly displayed. I didn't think I needed counseling then nor do I think that I need counseling now. However, I must concede that the events that transpired in Graham 203 represented emotional trauma that has resulted in a decisive change in teaching pedagogy.

A September to Remember

September 25, 2013 was a day like many other teaching days, except it turned out to be the worst day of my academic career. September 25, 2013 was a professional car wreck. It was the day I was informed that I was being accused of sexual harassment and racial discrimination.

My accusers were two white female students. A Title IX investigation was underway, and the original plan was that the Investigators would directly inform me. The Chair of the Sociology Department insisted that she be the one to break the news to me. There was a note on my door from the Department Chair requesting to see me. I did not think much of it so I casually walked into her office a little after lunch time. My African-American Social Thought class was scheduled to start at one o'clock. The meeting was anything but routine. The news broke my heart. I had been teaching for sixteen years up to that point, and did not cancel class when learning my mother had passed November 15, a Tuesday in 2011. I taught class the next day, Wednesday. This represented a different kind of hurt. I was stunned, and dizzy with disbelief. Before I knew it, I had started crying. I was not able to regain any composure while walking down the hall towards my office. I was devastated and I canceled class for the first time ever due to grief. I needed a moment to face my students so it was the Chair of the Department that actually went to inform the class of the cancellation.

I'm Eight Feet Deep!

I am innocent! Still it's amazing how confident innocence can be eroded by a five month long Title IX investigation for sexual harassment and racial discrimination. Swimming provided a way to escape the noise that accompanied what seemed to be a personal hell. One day during Thanksgiving Break, I found myself eight feet deep, sitting at the bottom of a swimming pool, crying! I didn't know it was possible to cry under water. The emotions were overwhelming and for a moment, I did contemplate just staying underwater. I knew it meant intentional drowning. An alternate voice chimed, "only the guilty would stay under water." I stood up and pushed to the surface, hearing one word on the way up, "daddy!" My daughter who was not physically present at the swimming pool had found a way to reach me. Upon surfacing and taking in air, chest aching, I proclaimed I would not give in, give up, nor give anymore tears to being falsely accused of sexual harassment and racial discrimination.

For reason of feeling ashamed, I did not disclose the fact that I was being investigated to any family, fraternity brothers or friends. Why does an innocent man feel ashamed? I always preached to my wife and daughter that we should not engage in anything that would bring our family name shame. Yet there I was the one who was bringing negativity to the family name and at that time, being innocent was irrelevant to the reality of being investigated. Although I was innocent, it still had to be proven that I did nothing wrong. Of course my colleagues knew because it had spread like wildfire within the department. Another reason for keeping it from family, fraternity brothers, and friends was that I knew there would be questions everyday about a process that I had no idea about how long it would take for the Deputy Investigator and Investigator to conclude.

Nearing the end of the investigation, I became exhausted so I reached out to Duck an Eleven Deuce Hoover from South Central, Los Angeles for counseling. At that time, I felt, I needed a different type of energy, and that is exactly what he provided. Ironically, Duck told me I had become too comfortable in a predominantly white society, and had let my guard down. I had failed to protect myself because of a false perception that there was no clear and present danger. Duck went on to say that I had become overly invested in the importance of the fame related to being one of the few black male professors on campus. He added that it was time to soldier up by sharpening the body (lifting weights), strengthening the mind (by reading and positioning everyone not family and fraternity brothers as the enemy) and feeding the spirit (by reading God's word). Duck emphatically encouraged me to become an unapproachable weapon, to realize that being black marks me for war, and that these charges represented war against me. I subscribed to his advice because it made sense and it seemed to reposition me as a conqueror and not a victim.

The Set-up: Class, Circumstance and Complaints

My primary responsibility in the Sociology Department is to offer courses in the criminology concentration (e.g., sociology of deviant behavior, juvenile delinquency, and contemporary gangs in America). Moreover, in an effort to counter the department's failure to exhaust the significance of the race variable and be inclusive of contributions by African-American scholars, I added elective courses, African-American Social Thought and African-American Perspectives on Crime to the sociology/criminology curriculum. African-American Social Thought was first taught during the spring 2003 session. The African-American Social Thought and African-American Perspectives on Crime courses have been routinely taught (as undergraduate courses) at least once per academic cycle since 2003.

African-American Social Thought was advertised (posted abstract) on the bulletin boards on the third floor of the Graham building where the Department of Sociology is located.

The abstract reads:

The legacy of the Black experience in America has a diverse narrative. This course fully embraces the reality that race is a social construction. This course will examine the value of blackness, the contextualization of black men as dangerous and in need of control, and that of black women as having no soul to be outraged. Are black men and women living and attempting to love one another having never truly escaped a legacy of existence in the American conscience as Predatory for him and Hottentot Venus for her? Does Black Love Have a Troubled Tradition attached to it when she is the Amazon and he is the Eunuch? It's been said that there is a thin line between love and hate. This course examines that "thin line" as existing within the duality of the American Dream and the American Nightmare. Advisory should be noted as the topics covered will not shy away from emotional discomfort as we will explore the depths of loving and hating blackness in America!

The fall 2013 semester began Wednesday August 19th, and somewhere between September 6th and September 13th two complaints, one of sexual harassment and one of racial discrimination had been filed in Student Affairs by two white females, who decided to by-pass the Chair of the Sociology Department. African-American Social Thought was taught in Graham 203, with seminar style seating (25 seats positioned around a table). A total of twenty three students were enrolled. There were ten black males, seven black females, three white females, two white males, and one Asian male.

Given, my teaching pedagogy became a source of contention, it is necessary to provide a brief overview of my approach. My teaching objective is geared towards teaching sociology in a manner that has life course applicability. Fundamentally, my goal is to relate theory, perspectives, and concepts to students' structural, economic, and cultural realities and/or immediate situational circumstances so that they identify with what they are learning.

The intensity of identification enhances retention and provides a sound foundation for a connection to larger sociological phenomenon, which forces them to move from the personally subjective frame of reference to a more social scientific standard of thought.

African-American Social Thought had been offered consistently over a decade and Eldridge Cleaver's controversial book *Soul on Ice* was required each time the course was offered. Cleaver's *Soul on Ice* was the primary source of the two white female students' complaints. Although I had been using Cleaver's *Soul on Ice* for a decade, I guess 2013 would be the year the book's content coupled with my lecturing became offensive enough to produce an official complaint. Given the content in Cleaver's *Soul on Ice* led to students' discomfort, providing a brief synopsis of Cleaver's *Soul on Ice* is warranted. *Soul on Ice* is Cleaver's attempt to slap the Omnipotent Administrator (White Man) in the face through writing a book that Cleaver thinks proves that he too is an intellectual brain and not just a menial task performing male. Yet, he does not shy away from the one characteristic afforded to him, the reality of his sexual ability to satisfy a white woman. Cleaver delves into the race, gender hierarchy whereby he places white women on the highest pedestal of being an ultra-feminine female, while simultaneously relegating black women to sub-feminine female status.

Style and Content Breeds Troubling Waters

When engaging students about course material, all students are given an equal opportunity to speak; however, some have to be prompted to speak, particularly in cases where they are asked to respond to how the material makes them feel and then what do you think about the material we have been discussing?

The purpose of this is to allow for comfortable conversation starting with emotion then transition to a more rigorous academic critical analysis. The crux of the matter in Cleaver's *Soul on Ice* seems to be his attempts to legitimize his personhood as a black male. He deliberately suggests that black men favor white women. However, black men by virtue of being positioned as a super-masculine menial, absent of intellectual currency fail to embrace black women as essential companions and are rebuffed by their sub-feminine qualities. Alternatively, black men are attracted to the epitome of freedom, white women. The controversial tone of the book is that Cleaver contends that even though white women are married to white men, they desire to fulfill a psychic connection to black men (Cleaver, 1968).

The following passages certainly stirs controversy:

> In proportion to the intensity of the Ultrafeminine's fear and feel of the ice is her psychic lust for the flame, for the heat of the fire: the Body. The Ultrafeminine, seeking sexual satisfaction, finds only physical exhaustion in the bed of the Omnipotent Administrator and the odds are against her finding psychic satisfaction there. Her "psychic bridegroom" is the Supermasculine Menial. Though she may never have had a sexual encounter with a Supermasculine Menial, she is fully convinced that he can fulfill her physical need. It will be no big thing for him to do since he can handle those Amazons down there with him....she is allured and tortured by the secret, intuitive knowledge that he, her psychic bridegroom can blaze through the wall of her ice, plum her psychic depths, test the oil of her soul, melt the iceberg in her brain, touch her inner sanctum, detonate the bomb of her orgasm, and bring her sweet release...The psychic bride of the Supermasculine Menial is the Ultrafeminine. She is his "dream girl." She, the delicate, weak; helpless Ultrafeminine, exerts a magnetic attraction upon him. When he compares her with his own woman, the strong, self-reliant Amazon, lust for her burns in his brain. (Cleaver, 1968, pp. 214–217)

I am disciplined enough to not inquire about intimacy within personal relationships, instead I focus on the culture of friendship building, mate selection, social networking, and then transition into how race and gender are experienced in America. During, classroom time and after allowing all students to respond to Cleaver's concept of the psychic bridegroom, I asked three white female students to get involved in the conversation by responding to "what do you think about Cleaver's psychic bridegroom concept?"

One white female student (a non-traditional older student) responded that Cleaver is a narcissist, while the other two remained silent. From that point I did not attempt to coerce them into responding. After being informed of the complaint, apparently my accusers felt encroached upon and uncomfortable discussing the material in Cleaver's book. Specifically, their complaint was that the material and my direct method of inquiry made them feel sexually uncomfortable. As it turns out their complaint to Student Affairs was based on the notion that I had specifically asked them "how does it feel to be with a black man?" Evidently somehow what I had asked with respect to Cleaver's concept of the psychic bridegroom was heard as an invasive inquiry into their sexual experiences with black men in particular.

Their second complaint was that I discriminated against them by calling them "white girls" and not calling them by name. Apparently, they took offense to being prompted to speak using race/gender terms. If I am guilty of anything it is for not learning 23 students' name fast enough to address them by name, instead I would often prompt all of my students with "how do my white and black male, and female students feel or think about the material being discussed?" Cleaver is unkind in his description of "white girls," which is why I attempted to soften the blow of the content. Sometimes in an effort to establish professor-to-student rapport, I would refer to black and white males and females as brothers and sisters, which is symbolically used to convey a unified family or so I thought. Cleaver equated white girls to Ogres, evil and witches.

The following passages allows for such a logical conclusion:

> As I pranced about, club in hand, seeking new idols to smash, I encountered really for the first time in my life, with seriousness, The Ogre, rising up before me in a mist. I discovered, with alarm, that the Ogre possessed a tremendous and dreadful power over me, and I didn't understand this power or why I was at its mercy. I tried to repudiate the Ogre, root it out of my heart as I had done God, Constitution, principles, morals, and values-but the Ogre had its claws buried in the core of my being and refused to let go. I fought frantically to be free, but the Ogre only mocked me and sank its claws deeper into my soul. I knew then that I had found an important key, that if I conquered the Ogre and broke its power over me I would be free. But I also knew that it was a race against time and that if I did not win I would certainly be broken and destroyed. I, a black man, confronted The Ogre—the white woman. (Cleaver, 1968, pp. 24–25)

Reflecting back, it appears that my accusers did not particularly like what Cleaver had to say about white women. For me to stand before the class and use race/gender terms instead of names, likely led to them feeling offended enough to include racial discrimination in their complaint to Student Affairs. I am just speculating on this point, I really don't know for certain why racial discrimination was included in the complaint. Essentially, as of September 25, 2013 an investigation for sexual harassment, and racial discrimination was launched because of pedagogy and the content of Cleaver's book.

Title IX: I Did Not See It Coming

My research interests includes gangsterism and deviant, criminal and violent subcultures. I employ an ethnographic method to examine gangs and the subculture of violence. In total I have been examining gangs and the subculture of violence for twenty years or at least sixteen years prior to the Title IX investigation. The type of research I do could be considered dangerous. I was always on guard for the potential of bodily harm when engaging in ethnography so I felt I had the necessary protections in place. I really was just on autopilot when it came to teaching. I felt so comfortable walking into the classroom with the type of confidence and command that I didn't feel a need to be guarded in anyway. In fact, I felt free in the classroom. I felt free to choose my reading material and lecture using a style that I thought would develop and improve students' intellectual currency. The irony is I often prayed for safe returns whether I was in South Central Los Angeles doing research on the Hoover Gang, or doing club security/body guarding at night clubs known for attracting violence. I can't think of one instance when I prayed for safety with respect to being a professor in a classroom; therefore, I was completely blindsided by a Title IX investigation.

On Wednesday September 25th, 2013, a little after the noon hour, I was informed of the complaint. I was dizzy, distraught, confused, and far too emotional to teach the African-American Social Thought Class scheduled to begin at one o'clock. It took no time for the class to be informed about the Title IX investigation. I really can't accurately say how that information got out so quickly. I remember a black female student kept knocking on my office door a little after one o'clock. She was so persistent that I answered. She was asking pointed questions about a class assignment and I was just answering more so off of memory. I really was concentrating on not crying in front of her but she probably noticed that my eyes were red from crying. I did manage to answer all of her questions and the meeting ended. Soon after I received an email from another black female student who offered her support for the appropriateness of the course content, and my lecturing style. My next visitor was a non-traditional white female student who was upset enough to have already gone over and met with student affairs and the Lead Investigator. I have no idea how she accessed that information and managed to set up an interview so fast. By Wednesday evening I had received an email detailing the support I was receiving from so many students. Friday September 27th, was my first day back in class and as you can imagine the only two empty seats were the two accusers (who had already dropped the course).

For the most part, I apologized for cancelling class, and I pleaded with the students to not retaliate. I started to lecture more about the nuances of teaching pedagogy with respect to being black on a predominantly white campus. I did not have to declare innocence given, my accusers had implied that the sexual harassment and racial discrimination had taken place during the very same lectures twenty one other students received. I made it through that day. One white male student came up to me, extended his hand and said, "I support you one hundred percent." Another white male student followed me to my office and detailed how the two accusers had approached him regarding the appropriateness of the book and lectures. He responded that "it's a sociology course and it is normal." He said they had maintained it was vulgar. Next up was another student, black female, who spoke about being approached by the accusers who asked her did she think the class was too sexual? To which she responded no, the "stuff is in the readings." Unfortunately, the accusing parties never once indicated their concern in class or through email, there simply was no communication about their emotional takeaways from the course. I couldn't remember their names nor what they looked like. In fact the only way that I figured out their names was by going back to my attendance sheets to determine who attended class the least and sure enough two names matched the student accusers.

I soon scheduled a meeting with the Deputy Title IX Coordinator and it felt more like an arraignment. I was informed about the specifics of the complaints and what the process would involve. Information gathering included me turning in a teaching philosophy, a course syllabus, passages from *Soul on Ice*, and the notes that were related to the lectures. Moreover, a sampling of students were called in to be interviewed. In an effort to be transparent, I turned over all emails that students had been sending me.

Never once did I encourage students to email me and I did instruct them to speak the truth even if it did not reflect well on me. I wanted students who were called to be interviewed to be genuine. During my initial meeting with the Title IX Deputy Coordinator, he implied that my eagerness to clear up the matter is a positive step; however, his job was to investigate and not take sides. He informed me that the investigation would not be quick, it will be thorough and that another Title IX Investigator will be at the next meeting.

I became really nervous when he inquired about using Cleaver. He stated that Cleaver was controversial in the mid to late 1970's and the book continues to "rub people the wrong way." He then suggested that when teaching, students hear differently, so was there any way possible that I could directly or indirectly be responsible for making students feel sexually harassed or racially discriminated against? I did not know what to say other than, "I am innocent," to which the Title IX Deputy Coordinator stated "the nature of the investigation will determine if you are." By this time, I am feeling uneasy because I did not feel that my innocence would be significant enough to neutralize the ingredients of being a black male, charged by two white females on a predominantly white campus. I quickly came to the conclusion that innocence is not the same as proving you did not do what your accusers say you did. Unfortunately, that is how the process made me feel, I felt that I had to win my innocence. On September 29th, I hand delivered a letter that detailed my teaching philosophy and the series of lectures that led to the students' complaints. I attached course outlines, dating back to 2003 as well as photocopies of Cleaver's book content, notes that all enrolled students had access to via our university canvas system, and end of the semester qualitative evaluations.

During, the second meeting with the Title IX Deputy Coordinator and Co-Investigator, I was far more assertive regarding my innocence. The Title IX Deputy Coordinator was professionally tough but the Co-Investigator, she was not only professionally tough, she was relentless. Although the Title IX Deputy Coordinator and Co-Investigator were black, taken together they represented this seemingly crucifying brick wall. I really felt like they were throwing darts at me, each one piercing my flesh. It was as if they were teaming up against me. The Title IX Deputy Coordinator sat to my right and the Co-Investigator sat behind this huge desk.

Questions came in rapid fire:

How did we get here? What role did you play? Did you single them out in any way? Did you call them white girls? What about asking them about sleeping with a black man? Was there any outside the classroom communication with them? How could two students feel the same way? What was their class attendance like? Were they good students? Did you ever violate their personal space? Have you had any personal conversations with them? Did they show you any signs of discomfort? Do you think it is possible that even with the best teaching intentions you may have unintentionally crossed the line with respect to verbally intruding upon their personal lives? Would you say that you treat all your students fairly? Shouldn't you have known your students' name by now?

The very same questions came in waves. I kept my composure but my anxiety level started to rise, I could feel my blood pushing through my veins, my head started throbbing, my throat started to hurt, and my eyes filled with water. I tried as best I could to make eye contact with both Investigators. I had answered each question as succinctly as possible, and yet I started to feel there is no way I will make it out of this interview without being found guilty. I no longer felt the interview was an information gathering session. I honestly felt the tide begin to shift in favor of substantiating the two white female students' claims of sexual harassment and racial discrimination but I still declared my innocence.

> I stated: I want to make it perfectly clear that I am innocent, I don't know why we are here and this represents a nightmare situation for my professional career. I am worried about my good name. I feel I have built an honest resume, been a faithful teacher with integrity and loyalty to the university. I feel I have served the department, college and university well. I want to make it perfectly clear, I don't recall ever receiving any form of communication from the students who have filed a complaint against me. By that I mean, I have never received or sent an email to either one of them nor have they expressed their discomfort to me about this class. Furthermore, I have never spoken to either student alone or together, in my office or in the hallway. I've never held any level of conversation with them outside of class about their personal lives or about this course. All communication has been in the classroom in clear view of their classmates. I have never come within five to ten feet of either one of them outside or inside of the classroom. The classroom is set up with a long seminar style table and I stand behind the technology station. It takes me some time to learn names of students and on those occasions when students stated their names before commenting on course content, the two accusing students were absent. I started my roll sheet after Labor Day and prior to that both students were routinely absent.

Just when I felt like I had addressed all of the questions, the Co-Investigator would start another round of asking the same questions but this time she asked me something that turned out to be emotionally overwhelming. The Co-Investigator asked "are you worried about your job?" It was at that point that I buried my head in my hands and cried. I spoke loudly to myself "Steve you promised you wouldn't do this, you promised." I can remember my legs shaking, my hands clinched in a fist. The tissue that was in my hand was so wet with tears that the tissue was nothing but lint. I was somewhere between hurt, embarrassed, and angry. I was not ever worried about my job, I was worried about being branded something dirty. I was worried about my good name.

I lifted my head from my hands, tears streaming down my face, looked the Co-Investigator in her eyes and I said, "I am innocent, I didn't do this, I don't care about my job, I will dig a ditch if I have to, I just want my good name back." I had nothing else left to say; however, the tears kept a steady flow. The Title IX Deputy Coordinator had gone to retrieve some tissue. Again I had dropped my head in tears. The Co-Investigator kept at it but this time I only offered that "I am innocent."

I felt foolish too because my tears were so heavy that the tissue had become too wet and had gotten all over my face. Thinking back, I felt weak, what kind of man was I to be openly displaying grief in front of strangers? I think even today, I am embarrassed that I cried in front of them. I had cried in front of a black man and committed the cultural sin of crying in front of a black woman. Both Investigators pivoted to aftermath advice. They were saying that no matter the results of the investigation that I could not let this be a defining moment of failure but more of learning and emerging a better professor because of lessons learned. I thought I was really in trouble at that point. The Co-Investigator offered one more piece of advice, she suggested that I seek emotional counseling because of the toll that the investigation was obviously taking on me. My immediate response was "I don't need counseling, I will just pray and keep praying."

The meeting had come to a close, I thanked the Deputy Coordinator and Co-Investigator. I did not shake their hands because my palms were wet. I asked could I exit the back door and they agreed. I did not want to have to walk through a lobby to exit the building. I was embarrassed that I had cried in front of two strangers. I felt I violated some ghostly code of masculinity that black men don't cry in public or in front of people. As I walked towards my car, I looked up to the sky and simply murmured "where were you when I needed you?" I was a troubled man facing troubling times and I wanted my God to know it.

Time Stands Still When Waiting on a Verdict

It was a university Title IX investigation, an information gathering opportunity to hear all sides but for me, it felt like I was on trial. I became aware that the investigation was underway on September 25, 2013, and I did not receive any indication of a decision until December 4th, 2013. On December 4th, 2013, the Title IX Deputy Coordinator intimated via email that the investigation was concluding and that I could relax and enjoy the Holidays. I was not altogether sure what that meant but at least it was positive news. Prior to December 4th, 2013, I would only come to campus to teach, leaving soon after my classes. There was no way I wanted interaction with any students, graduate or undergraduate, especially white female students. As the investigation wore on, all of my students had been classified as the enemy. I was not thinking about how to effectively teach. I was thinking "how can I get away from these demons without offending them?" In my mind, every student represented the next potential accuser, and I wanted nothing to do with any of them. I had spent countless hours reliving my lectures, trying to identify where I could have possibly gone wrong. I had settled on Cleaver's book being controversial with respect to race and sexuality but at the same time, I thought about how I had been using *Soul on Ice* for a decade.

I immediately stopped going to department meetings because I did not want to be a distraction. My colleagues in the department were supportive as they could be but none of them had answers outside of having to wait to see what the investigation revealed. However, when the formal decision came down, I decided to pen an open letter to the department and each faculty member.

My fall and Thanksgiving Breaks were a blur. A few events stand out. Holding back tears when in the presence of my wife and daughter, and keeping my ordeal away from my family. Crying in Walmart and at stop lights. Swimming and sitting eight feet deep in a Sport's Complex swimming pool contemplating giving up. There is no dancing around the issue, I had suicidal thoughts. Trading in my Chevy Suburban for a less visible Chevy Traverse because I wanted to be less noticeable. Full disclosure, I wanted a brand new vehicle because I felt dirty. I mean after all, I was being accused and had not been cleared of behavior that was wicked. I wanted to leave the predominantly white institution and seek refuge at a historically black university.

In March of 2014, I received two official memorandums (one for each accuser) dated February 26, 2014 from the Title IX Coordinator, concerning Title IX of the Education Amendments of 1972 and title VI of the Civil Rights Act of 1964 Investigation Closure. The memorandum stated:

> The investigators concluded that the allegations were unsubstantiated and did not involve prohibitions under Title IX of the Education Amendments of 1972 or Title VI of the Civil Rights act of 1964.....Witness testimony substantiated expectations initially communicated to all students in the African-American Social Thought course regarding content, scope, and pedagogical purpose. The preponderance of evidence does not substantiate allegations of sexual harassment or race discrimination and that opportunity to drop the course based on course content, scope, and pedagogical purpose was communicated to all African-American Social Thought students during the first week of class.

Essentially, I was held hostage by an investigation that lasted approximately five months. I am thankful that the decision matched the truth! I was innocent. I am innocent. Nevertheless, the process indirectly seemed to punish me for being accused. The duration produced emotions that kept me depressed. I was trouble minded at the time, so much so that I even questioned whether God was paying attention. The truth did prevail but the truth did not come without me experiencing emotional trauma.

As for my two accusers. I don't think I ever hated them. If I could ask them one question, it would be "why me?" It has been a little over four years since the initial complaint and investigation and I am still coping with some side effects. Fundamentally, I have morphed into a cautious professor as opposed to one that enthusiastically embraces classroom instruction.

The Godly thing to do is to forgive. I have not done that and I do not think I can forgive them for accusing me of sexual harassment and racial discrimination. Honestly, what they did, hurt me. Perhaps they do not care and have moved on. It does not matter to me one way or the other. Their claims were baseless, and I endured a process that vindicated me.

As a result, I am neutral when I think about them now. I do not wish them well, and I do not wish them harm. I no longer have pure joy of teaching. I yield to being satisfied with getting through lectures without being offensive. My immediate goal is to not have another Title IX complaint, which prohibits my genuine pedagogical style. The most profound statement the Deputy Coordinator said to me after the case had been closed was "you have got to survive on this campus." I knew what he meant. In fact, my lectures are extremely measured and censored. I have not used Cleaver's book since then, and I record my lectures. I was totally consumed by the Title IX investigation, and I will never get back the time I lost. The professor that I am now will never be as good as the professor I used to be prior to the Title IX investigation.

· 3 ·

DU BOIS' SOULS OF
BLACK AND WHITE FOLK

Can't Out Run Caste in America

Public opinion concerning the progress of blacks since the Emancipation Proclamation endorsed by Lincoln in 1863, some 155 years ago seems to be captured by the question, what is up with a race of people who show slow signs of progress given they were freed 155 years ago? True freedom never materialized with the Emancipation Proclamation as evidenced by continued oppression. The record continues to show that the Civil Rights' Era produced better lifestyle opportunities, yet better did not mean equal. Therefore, the black condition is still one of critical immediacy to conditions that restrict better life course outcomes. When the argument that blacks should be further along because of freedoms afforded approximately 155 years ago is allowed to fill the social air without thorough examination, we are left with a false narrative that blacks must be inferior. It is far too simplistic to coin white people as having sole responsibility when in reality white people are one component of a complex social structure that is the system (e.g., capitalism, social regulation, social hierarchies, cultural contexts, etc.). Social sciences (taken to mean Sociology and Psychology) and notable media outlets or vessels of information dissemination (directly or indirectly) have historically fueled contentions that blacks are inferior. In fact, those thought to be inferior become defined by the superior class and racial success or socially acceptable legitimacy is only possible through integration (Jones, 1973). According to the grass roots Black Power Movement, integration siphons the best that a race has to offer while forcing the perceived negative characteristics to be marginalized and this is done through exploitation, cultural imposition, and co-optation. Social sciences have been responsible for institutional policy and political alignments that appear to contribute to whites engaging in a God Complex (sitting in judgment of blacks) and casting dispersions that amount to labeling and channeling social mobility and cultural options (Ture and Hamilton, 1992).

Social sciences are guilty of presenting a social record of blacks in comparison to whites (using whites as a social judgment scale) and then arguing that blacks' life course outcomes are fundamentally contextualized by moral depravity (sex code practices and criminality) and fundamental failures (less than ideal cultural habits bordering on depravity, intellectual erosions, not being able to transcend pseudo traumas related to slavery, and/or declining from the ability to build and maintain solid families) to the point that black people are deserving of being subjected to oppression. Additionally, brokers of racial power dynamics in-capsulate blacks into the proverbial catch 22/ damned if you do/damned if you don't argument with respect to blacks' rage versus forgiveness. This very same catch 22 vacuum has been used to divide the civil rights non-violent movement from the black nationalists, grass roots black power approach, even though they shared similar goals (Jones, 1973; Ture and Hamilton, 1992).

Racial casting remains pervasive signaling that blacks are still subject to traditional stereotypes that attempt to socially construct blackness as having character deficits and underlying depravity. Black men became wicked as a side effect of American overt hate and indifference regarding equitable humanity. The all too common cliché professing not to see color fails to grasp the meaning of blackness in America. Du Bois prophetically offered that American race relations would continue to be beset by problematic racial appraisals. Despite America's creed, its collective practice has a record of negating the humanity of blackness. For the past 575 years (dating back to 1444 to 2019) blacks have contended with being labelled property and tertium quid, have had their black manhood categorically denied and relegated to being existentially absurd, suffered a collective fearful gaze as if looking at an unpredictable animal, and are currently contending with value of life differentials (Du Bois, 1953; Dyson, 1996; Glaude, 2016; Gray, 1995; Wilson, 2009; West, 2001).

Radical sociology dares to examine the authentic differences of marginalized groups in America. Radical sociology explores the roots of freedom by way of emancipation and liberation. Radical sociology lays before us valuable intellectual currency that is produced from the struggle for equitable humanity. According to Flacks and Turkel (1978) knowledge is a key ingredient to emancipation. For Flacks and Turkel (1978), fundamentally it is knowledge that helps identify, focus and locate experiences, discontents, and troubles as aspects of processes that are subject to human intervention and transformation. "Such knowledge rests on the assumption that the significant constraints on human action are man-made and/or subject to change through conscious human effort" (Flacks and Turkel, 1978, pp. 193–194). Radical sociology is inherently equipped to address socially constructed racial hierarchies in a democratic, money market society. It logically follows that radical sociology, a non-mainstream sociological approach contributed to the development of black sociology, especially when radical sociology addressed issues of power, protest, and the pursuit of existential freedom within the context of restrictive political systems (Flacks and Turkel, 1978). Standing on its own merits, black sociology extends radical sociology because it presumes critical differences in lived experiences between blacks and whites in America. Du Bois, developed black sociology during a reluctant academic climate that seemed to oppose a research agenda that concentrated on blackness as more than second class citizens. In fact it is fair to suggest that white academics, philanthropists and culturalists did not place much value on the transformative realities experienced by American Negros from slavery to freedom (Wright II and Calhoun, 2006).

> Du Bois' persisted: (1) if the Negroes are not ordinary human beings, if their development is simply the retrogression of an inferior people, and the only possible future for the Negro, a future of inferiority, decline and death, then it is manifest that a study of such a group, while still of interest and scientific value is of less pressing and immediate necessity than the study of a group which is distinctly recognized as belonging to the great human family, whose advancement is possible, and whose future depends on its own efforts and the fairness and reasonableness of the dominant and surrounding group; and (2) it is of course perfectly clear as to why scientific men have long fought shy of [the study of Black Americans]. The presence of the Negro in America has long been the subject of bitter and repeated controversy-of war and hate, of strife and turmoil. It has been said that so dangerous a field, where feelings were deep-seated and turbulent, was not the place for scientific calm of clear headed investigation (Du Bois [1904] 1978, pp. 56–57, from Wright II and Calhoun, 2006, p. 3).

Does Du Bois have a handle on America by way of providing auto-ethnographic commentary on the souls of black and white folk? This chapter reexamines and extends, Du Bois' discussion on the souls of black and white folk by exploring his critical comments that arrests the souls of white folk, convicting them to racial intolerance, religious selfishness and murderous insecurity.

Du Bois states: high in the tower, where I sit above the loud complaining of human sea. I know many souls that toss and whirl and pass, but none there are that intrigue me more that the Souls of White Folk. Of them I am singularly clairvoyant. I see in and through them, I view them from unusual points of vantage. Not as a foreigner do I come for I am native, not foreign, bone of their thought and flesh of their language. Mine is not the knowledge of the traveler or the colonial composite of dear memories, words and wonder. Nor yet is my knowledge that which servants have of masters or mass of class or capitalist of artisan. Rather I see these souls undressed and from the back and side. I see the working of their entrails. I know their thoughts and they know that I know. This knowledge makes them now embarrassed, now furious! They deny my right to live and be and call me misbirth! My word is to them mere bitterness and my soul, pessimism. And yet as they preach and strut and shout and threaten, crouching as they clutch at the rags of facts and fancies to hide their nakedness, they go twisting, flying by my tired yes and I see them ever stripped-ugly, human. (Du Bois, 1920, p. 453)

Comments from Frederick Douglas, Marcus Garvey, Alexander Crummell, Malcolm X, Michael Eric Dyson, Cornel West, and Eddie Glaude will be examined to further determine how black men have been culturally regarded over time.

The social construction of black masculinity from Douglas through Glaude reveals fluid cultural meanings that are at times disturbing, dismissive, perplexing, offensive, degrading, anchored in negativity, void of humanity, distanced from spirituality, non-deserving of civility, destined for character assaults, and representative of a contested existence with fleeting redemptive values. As early as Douglas' offering of the socially constructed slave and progressively moving towards a supposed post racial society marked by Glaude's race value gap perspective, I wonder about this country's ability to be reflexive enough to critically examine its racial legacy. The bloodlines of blacks and whites are intertwined and yet severing them appears to be America's great past time. Frederick Douglas considers the blood of Africans within the context of slavery. The institution of slavery justified human order, human dominion, and right of social control regulation, positioning, punitive consequences and barbaric cruelty. Frederick Douglas contends that slavery martyrs humanity removing slaves from the equitable personhood designed and owed to them by virtue of being made in the image of God.

Douglass states: It is only when we contemplate the slave as a moral and intellectual being, that we can adequately comprehend the unparalleled enormity of slavery, and the intense criminality of the slaveholder. I have said that the slave was a man. What a piece of work is a man! How noble in reason! How infinite in faculties! In form and moving how express and admirable! In action how like an angel! In apprehension how like God! The beauty of the world! The paragon of animals! The image of God, but a little lower than the angels; possessing a soul, eternal and inde-structible; capable of endless happiness, or immeasurable woe; a creature of hopes and fears, of affections and passions, of joys and sorrow and he is endowed with those mysterious powers by which man soars above the things of time and sense, and grasps, with undying tenacity the elevating and sublimely glorious idea of God. It is such a being that is smitten and blasted. The first work of slavery is to mar and deface those characteristics of its victims which distinguish men from things and persons from property. Its first aim is to destroy all sense of high moral and religious responsibility. (Brotz, 1966,p. 217)

Slavery as an institution removed blacks from discussions of having a soul that is redeemable, creating a spiritual blind spot and distancing from God, which alternatively created room to inject notions that the Africans in their natural state were demonic and unholy possessing animality that cast them outside the religious universe (Cannon, 2004).

Additionally, slavery is befitting of Africans as state property, by reason of race slavery represents God's plan for the slave and lynching is sufficient for the irredeemable souls of Africans (Raper, 1933). Although slavery has ended as an economic and labor institution, American institutions like the criminal justice system, educational system, and life chance opportunity systems con-tinue to wage a campaign that highlights racial differences.

In his appeal to the soul of white America, Garvey attempted to capture the attention of whites who had sympathy for the condition of blacks. Garvey was convinced that whites had a solution to the race problem that ranged on a continuum of extermination, legalized oppression, and equal segregation in a nation of their own. Garvey's position is based on the assumption that a minority of whites with a sensible conscious has at times conceded to the prevailing theme of oppression, which leads Garvey to state:

Negroes are human beings-the peculiar and strange opinions of writers, ethnologies, philosophers, scientists, and anthropologist notwithstanding. They have feelings, souls, passions, ambitions, desires, just as other men, hence they must be considered. Has white America really considered the Negro in the light of permanent human progress? The answer is NO. (Brotz, 1966, p. 556)

The black experience has included attempts at extermination, legalized oppression and segregation so this country has applied many forms of regula-tion and control that was inherently racist. A core ingredient of the ongoing intra-racial civil war is the perpetual resistance to Garvey's answering "no" to whether white America really considers progressive, successful black people.

The black experience in this country has produced class stratification, differences in economic, religious, cultural and social ideologies, as well as political variation that has created intra-racial enemies with secret misgivings and desires to see the permanent black underclass cannibalize itself until extinction leaving those judged to be successful to serve as race credits.

Yes, pockets of black America seek racial accreditation from white America. Less by nationalistic independence and more by competitive integration. This segment of black America has successfully subscribed to and invested in the American Dream, which soothes mainstream America's conscience leading to believing that past racial atrocities have been rectified.

The manic hiccup of racial oppression was reflective of generational fears passed down from a prior generation that were themselves beholden to delusional preoccupations of African depravity. The matter of concern regarding treatment of blacks at that time was situationally reasonable whenever and wherever preoccupations were anchored by the perspective that righteous men were entitled to protect families and way of life from persons thought to be vessels of harm. Time has been the remedy for racial intolerance due to periods of social movements that bolstered personhood enlightenment whereby relative equitable humanity replaced racial distancing.

For some the veil, (skin tone) indicative of an unpredictable unknown creature had fallen and in its place stood a different kind of black man. A more tolerable one. Pluralistic integration has positive returns affirming the value of meritocracy and patriotism in America. Black excellence, cultural integration and mutual legacy forgiveness or a mutual willingness to sidestep uncomfortable conversations about negative inter-racial experiences has bread Race Men, and New Black Aesthetics (Boyd, 1997).

The black experience that pre-dates the civil rights movement has faded as a talking point, replaced by a level of black excellence that refuses association with an ancestry victimized by white manifest destiny. Black Race Men and New Black Aesthetics seemed engaged in successful integration only holding course on a palpable level of discourse about race when interacting in inter-racial settings. Harmony of thought between these Race Men, New Black Aesthetics and white America is best achieved by convincing one another that the dangerous racial holdout is the disgruntled, disenfranchised, marginalized, permanent underclass black who is in fact the modern day class of niggaz. These so called "niggaz" are a credible threat and are a danger to universal civility and functional citizenship. Furthermore, there is no intra-racial allegiance between black Race Men, New Black Aesthetics, and niggaz

(Boyd, 1997; Du Bois, 1953; Hernandez, 2014; Love and Tosolt, 2014; West, 2001; Wilson, 2009). Instead black pride from the revisionist black conservative is recognized through successful integration and inter-racial coalitions more than subscribing to permanent underclass residents who continue to encounter economic, legal, cultural, and social hardships. Revisionist black conservatives still represent competition for comparable socially mobile white America so the veil, while not primary, remains at a shouting distance, still significant enough to conjure suspicion and concern from white America.

Self-appointed black political leaders resembling race effacing characteristics have emerged to fill the void of suspicion, earning the trust of white constituents and white liberals by dismissing them from racial legacy entanglements. Countering race effacing black leaders are the protest leaders who seem limited to racial turfs and can't quite navigate the racial transcending minefield enough to engage in inter-racial coalitions.

This is where the race transcending prophetic type leaders emerge to seemingly attempt to grip black racial authenticity steeped in grass roots communities, and override the nuances of racial divisions enough to appear a pleasant compromise or departure from "status hungry black political leaders." Race-transcending leadership is of "highest demand" in the public sphere (West, 2001, pp. 60–61).

When the politics of race becomes a burden too much to bear, there is a pivot towards black intellectuals. Black intellectuals have concentrated on their respective disciplines, which more often than not does not involve ethnographic research or enough immediate observations to decode the pulse of all Black America. Still there is some level of confidence in their intellectual currency, which may be middle class specific in focus thereby medicating white America by feeding their ignorance over assuming that Race Men, New Black Aesthetics, and status hungry black political leaders represent enough of a conservative movement to assume all is well enough to not feel nor think about the plight of black men in society (Dyson, 1997; West, 2001). The news flash here is that not all black intellectuals, even the most trusted, most visible on media outlets represent the pulse of black America. More specifically, those black intellectuals who invest more in secondary data points more than a Chicago style return to the field for information gathering, are representative of temporary pulse checkers and not substantive knowledge vessels.

Dyson state: The enhanced currency of black public intellectuals also rides the wave of popularity that sections of black life are enjoying. If there's one fact of black life in white America we can't deny it; it is this, black folk go in and out of style. Most of the time our identities are exploited for white commercial ends, or ripped off to further the careers of white imitators. Blackness is today a hot commodity; but of course it always has been: the selling of black bodies on the slave market, minstrel shows, Elvis's cloning of black gospel blues singers all point to the fetish of black skin and skill in American popular culture. Once the barriers to black achievement were lowered, black folk ourselves got more of the fat. Black bodies are "in" now, that is, if you don't happen to be a black man with a car, tangling with the police in Los Angeles or the white suburbs of Pittsburgh. (Dyson, 1997, p. 53)

I am a black man in America; therefore, I am haunted by a unique race legacy and hunted because I am a member of a group that continues to occupy mainstream America's collective conscience as someone to be feared and/or different enough to arouse suspicion, and concern for other's safety. The sociologist in me wonders in spite of racial progress: (1) how is it possible to be haunted by a troublesome racial legacy faced by my ancestors that was supposed to be made "equitable and equal" by a civil rights movement? and (2) how is it possible to have been hunted and/or my personhood contested via civil inequality, character assassinations, and false accusations that lead to a Title IX investigation on a university campus, and discretionary practices with respect to encounters with police officers?

My research publications, and teaching interest spans 21 years covering the race variable with respect to crime, arrests, victimization, discretionary justice, arrests rates, education, class stratification, social movements, culture and subcultural formations, gangsterism, and inter and intra-racial relationships. Coupled with my lived experiences, I find that four narratives still resonate. First, Du Bois suggests that black men contend with afterthoughts related to social forces that enslave the spirit, regulate behaviors and force submission to un-natural dominion of one race over another (Du Bois, 1953).

Du Bois states: And last of all there trickles down that third and darker thought,-the thought of the things themselves, the confused, half-conscious mutter of men who are black and whitened, crying "Liberty, Freedom, Opportunity-vouchsafe to us, O boastful World, the chance of living men!" To be sure, behind the thought lurks the afterthought, suppose, after all, the World is right and we are less than men? Suppose this mad impulse within is all wrong, some mock mirage from the untrue?. (Du Bois, 1953, p. 75)

Second, Alexander Crummell, contends that communities are often perplexed by racial problems when differing races attempt to coexist equitably. Historically, people of different stock engage in behaviors that seek extinction, or complete segregation.

In cases of social mingling there are attempts to dominate via antagonistic race relations, preferential assimilation, exploitation, cultural imposition, and co-optation, and perhaps be perpetually engaged in blood mixture conflict and race ranking. For Crummell, there is an undercurrent resistant temperament towards authentic existentialism in a society that deems one race as superior and the other inferior (Brotz, 1966).

> Crummell states: But just here the case spirit interferes in this race-problem and declares: You Negroes may get learning; you may get property; you may have churches and religion, but this is your limit! This is a white man's Government! No matter how many millions you may number, we Anglo-Saxons are to rule! This is the edict constantly hissed in the Negro's ear, in one vast section of the land. (Brotz, 1966, p. 188)

Both Du Bois and Crummell's writings seem to imply that blacks' relative success in this country has been tempered by a veil that continues to symbolize a racial threat and; therefore, should never depart from the eyes of suspicion and caution. Black conservatives shout from roof tops, the America of old is dead! There are no civil rights that are out of the reach of black people. There is nothing standing in the way of blacks' success. Nothing out of the ordinary or specialized trap doors exist that circumvents blacks' earnest attempts at seizing upon life chance advancements. Whatever tangible and/ or intangible resources and commodities that were once forbidden are now accessible. For them, a white man's world or a white man's government is outdated and contemporarily irrelevant. Pivoting back to the black conservative think tank relative to regarding an America fixated on a white man's government, these very same black conservatives would be hard pressed to deny that they have not engaged in race work, code switched and/or put on race neutral masks to accommodate the whites in their business networks and social circles (Glaude, 2016; Wilson, 2009).

The black conservative train of thought is a strict class argument and fails to consider the impact of racial casting; therefore, it is logical to move on to casting consequences. There are significant side effects related to a troublesome race legacy. Africans who became black in America were subjected to a European gaze that inherently constructed a racial social hierarchy that placed a specific class of black people at the bottom of the socioeconomic scale. Consequently some blacks become singularly focused on the market culture. Pursuing class status at the expense of racial authenticity, refuge at the expense of salvation, individualism at the expense of brother and sisterhood, and calculative self-serving exchanges at the expense of a measured degree of humility.

> Du Bois states: In the Black World, the Preacher and Teacher embodied once the ideals of this people, the strife for another and a juster world, the vague dream of righteousness, the mystery of knowing; but to-day the danger is that these ideals, with their simple beauty and weird inspiration, will suddenly sink to a question of cash and lust for gold. (DuBois, 1953, p. 68)

> West states: Living a "random now lifestyle" fortuitous and fleeting moments preoc-cupied with getting over, acquiring pleasure, property, and power by any means nec-essary. Post-modern culture is more and more a market culture dominated by gangster mentalities and self-destructive wantonness (immoral behavior). This culture engulfs all of us, yet its impact on the disadvantaged is devastating, resulting in extreme violence in everyday life. Sexual violence against women and homicidal assaults by young black men on one another are only the most obvious signs of this empty quest for pleasure, property, and power (West, 2001, p. 10).

What does it say about race relations when we seem to remain fixed on the permanent underclass of blacks (which has fewer households than working, middle, and upper classes), as the primary driver for manufactured fear about criminality, family dysfunction, social affiliations, racial conformity, cultural appraisals, human life value adjustments, caste and race ranking, and/or the general assumption that blacks continue to represent some form of a social health hazard? The result is that the permanent underclass, while being in the minority of black households in America has the largest social fingerprint that drives the negative racial narratives in this country.

Moreover, this very same permanent underclass continues to effect neg-ative race relations in America. It is almost as if the black upper and middle classes exist in obscurity except for the fact that black males in these classes continue to be beholden to the very same social estimations endured by per-manent underclass black males.

As far as the permanent underclass is concerned, there is the problem that there seems to be a relative degree of subscribing to embracing failure by refusing to accept personal responsibility and giving into the nefarious devices in the immediate environment and/or adopting the cool pose. Newton argues that black males residing in resource strained and socially declining enclaves have a keen ability to decipher the nature of their oppression but lack reason-able sophistication to transcend oppression and therefore fall victim to ac-cepting failure and behavioral pathologies that indicate inferiority (Hilliard, Zimmerman, and Zimmerman, 2006).

The fourth social narrative that continues to resonate, is adopting a cool pose. According to Majors and Billson (1992), black males residing in urban areas cope with the prospects of social status failures, and lack of success in mainstream, educational and job arenas by subscribing to a nonchalant cool presentation of self. Any circumstances that contest their black masculinity is countered by giving no hint of being negatively affected by the pressure that is associated with failure. It appears that the cool pose is primary in delivering a status equalizer even when failure is eminent (Hall, 2009; Majors and Billson, 1992).

When considering the contextual pressures imposed on black masculinity, it is not hard to imagine that black men can be conflicted by insecurity because of contested manhood, and adverse casting consequences leading to alienation. It therefore is possible to be haunted by ascription of black manhood that is deemed threatening.

Additionally, it is a fact that by virtue of being a black male, I too have dealt with being hunted, singled out, and positioned as dangerous for no other reason except being black and male. I exist in some circles as a newly promoted Full Professor at a predominantly white institution, the first black male in the department's 104 year history. My tenure there has been a mixture of professional success that was often countered by erasing the joy of that success because of racial undertones. Moreover, I am a survivor of a Title IX investigation that was about teaching pedagogy, and race, gender and power dynamics that resulted in a self-imposed censorship. My encounters with the police continue to be reflective of race cultural regalia related to my black skin and has nothing to do with my social mobility. I am alive simply because I am fortunate that I have not encountered a police officer who misunderstood my demeanor to be a threat. The reality is that my life is a negotiation when encountering a police officer. I am far beyond imagining race as a calling card for my experiences because I have lived them and know that race is my master status over anything else.

A general take away is that whites (more so than blacks) have been able to experience full assimilation in the sense that America has favored white citizenship as the epitome of the righteous majority enough to offer better opportunities to embrace the American creed of life, liberty and the pursuit of happiness. Whites for the most part have become accustomed to accepting the advantages of preferential treatment, favored status, and/or the kind of white privilege (a skin toned credit card) that affords better life course outcomes, while denying the adverse racial implications for black people. It is reassuring to believe that investment in securing opportunities (more than white privilege) is significantly related to life chances (Wilson, 2009).

It is uncomfortable to think institutional race restrictions are discretely supported by family members. How disheartening is it that white kids attend colleges, and/or engage the world only to discover that their willingness to interact in diverse social circles alternatively exposes them to the racial sins of their parent and/or great grand-parents? Certainly, progressive racial interactions, inclusive of initiatives for inclusivity and diversity in schools and workplaces, and interacting in diverse social networks by virtue of social media and being actively involved in coalitions that confront racial injustices has worked to enhance the spirit of democracy, bolstered the power of individualism and the protest spirit. These are essential ingredients that seems on its face to erase notions of governing by race more than governing by core principles of human decency and deservedness (Brotz, 1966).

> Alexander Crummell states: they forget the Church of God is in the world; that her mission is by the Holy Ghost, to take the weak things of the world to confound the mighty, to put down the might from their seats, and to exalt them of low degree; that now, as in all the ages, she will, by the Gospel, break up tyrannies and useless dynasties, and lift up the masses to nobleness of life and exalt the humblest of men to excellence and superiority. Above all things, they forget the King invisible, immortal, eternal is upon the throne of the universe; that thither caste and bigotry , and race hate can never reach; that He is everlasting committed to the interests of the oppressed; that He is constantly sending forth succors and assistances for the rescue of the wronged and injured; that He brings all the forces of the universe to grind to powder all the enormities of earth, and to rectify all the ills of humanity, and so hasten on the day of universal brotherhood. By the presence and the power of that Divine Being all the alienations and disseverances of men shall be healed; all the race-problems of this land easily be solved; and love and peace prevail among men. (Brotz, 1966, pp. 189–190)

Crummell hinted that the problem with race in America is related to the difference between what religious affirmations we are mindful of with respect to how democratic freedoms work to topple traditional government restrictions. Such a sharp cleavage between the American creed, practice and religious freedoms become ingredients for a social, economic, cultural, and spiritual war.

It seems illogical on the surface to concede that the collective conscience of mainstream America includes the Church of God in a democratic society. However, it is plausible that El-Hajj Malik El-Shabazz (Malcolm X) discovered that Christian Gospel did factor into the society's collective conscience.

Malcolm X was a notable Muslim Nationalist figure that garnered attention in the form of death threats, uneasiness, and even fear of him being a secular Messiah/Commander for Black Muslims and grass roots groups who were priming for a racial war. Malcolm X stated that while many letters from whites were of the threatening and Dear "Nigger X" variety, for the most part letters exposed fears of intra-racial intimacy and that "God wrathfully is going to destroy this civilization" (Haley, 1964, 290).

While it is evident that African-Americans' socioeconomic status has improved and that permanent underclass households do not out number working, middle-class and well-to-do households, it is also evident that there has been a common thread of social identity distinction (casting) that has been allowed to survive since 1619 in a manner that serves to socially rank races. Therefore, it is beneficial to discuss Du Bois' souls of black and white folk to gauge where this country is with respect to labeling black males. More specifically, what is it about being black that factors into the most significant life course situations and outcomes. Is it my life in America or is it my black life in America?

> Du Bois states: The Negro is a sort of seventh son, born with a veil and gifted with second-sight in this American world, a world which yields him no true self-consciousness, but only lets him see himself through the revelation of the other world. It is a peculiar sensation, this double-consciousness, this sense of always looking at ones' self through the eyes of others, of measuring one's soul by the tape of a world that looks on in amused contempt and pity. One ever feels his twoness,-An American, a Negro; two souls, two thoughts, two unreconciled strivings; two warring ideals in one dark body, whose dogged strength alone keeps it from being torn asunder (Du Bois, 1953, pp. 16–17).

It is relevant to resurrect Du Bois' souls of black folk because this country has continued to function as if a racial value gap exists, which emphatically impedes reasonable solutions to perceived confrontational conflicts that place racial reverence of life in competition (Glaude, 2016). The relentlessness of existing in a double-consciousness, which implies being denied racial authenticity and replaced with contested blackness is stressful, troublesome and heightens racial tensions (Estes, 2005; Wilson, 2009). Blacks are then forced to look at themselves with some great consideration of how others see them.

> Du Bois states: Between me and the other world there is ever an un-asked question: unmasked by some through feelings of delicacy; by others through difficulty of rightly framing it. All nevertheless, flutter round it. They approach me in a half-hesitant sort of way, eye me curiously or compassionately, and then, instead of saying directly,

How does it feel to be a problem? They say, I know an excellent colored man in my town...Do these Southern outrages make your blood boil? At these I smile, or am interested, or reduce the boiling to a simmer, as the occasion may require. To the real question, how does it feel to be a problem? I answer seldom a word (DuBois, 1953, p. 15).

Du Bois contends that blacks have a sense of the importance of their racial heritage and the benefits of remaining authentically true to tribal lineage. Meaning, Du Bois argues that it is simultaneously possible to integrate without completely conceding to that idea that there are parts about blackness that is better eliminated.

Du Bois states: He would not bleach his Negro soul in a flood of white Americanism, for he knows that Negro blood has a message for the world. He simply wishes to make it possible for a man to be both a Negro and an American, without being cursed and spit upon by his fellows, without having doors of opportunity closed roughly in his face. (DuBois, 1953, p. 17)

There is considerable chatter about the value of blackness. Moreover, there is still evidence that the black body disproportionately contends with lethal predation both intra-racially via black-on-black crime and over-zealous law enforcement agents. Blacks through continued racial casting continue to experience a direct assault on the sacred and the secular self, which penetrated the inner most thoughts of the humanity of blackness.

West states: No other people have been taught systematically to hate themselves-psychic violence-reinforced by the powers of the state and civic coercion-physical violence-for the primary purpose of controlling their minds and exploiting their labor for nearly four hundred years. (West, 2001, p. XIII)

Can this country be accused of continuing to engage in systematically teaching blacks to hate themselves? If not, then why does a value gap exist between blacks and whites promoting white lives as more valuable than blacks? Moreover, what about the negative afterthoughts that blacks have had to contend with (Du Bois, 1953)? Can it be said that these thoughts are no longer relevant?

Du Bois states: The second thought streaming from the death-ship and the curving river is the thought of the older South-the sincere and passionate belief that somewhere between men and cattle, God created a tertium quid and called it a Negro,-a clownish, simple creature, at times, even lovable within its limitations, but straitly foreordained to walk within the Veil. To be sure, behind the thought lurks the afterthought, -some of them with favoring chance might become men, but in sheer self-defence we dare not let them and we build about them walls so high and hang between them and the light a veil so thick that they shall not even think of breaking through. (Du Bois, 1953, pp. 74–75)

Does not an existence of a racial value gap indicate that although the integrationist agenda has provided life chance advances, there is a cultural lag in personhood appraisals that persists in some form? Du Bois' *Souls of Black Folk* describes race casting during the early 1900's. I contend that Du Bois remains accurate with respect to his perspectives on the souls of black folk even in light of America's 44th President, a black man named Barack Obama. President Obama is in many respects a political figure that comes close to a race-transcending profit, even though his political agenda seemed pro-socialist with respect to conceptualizing America as a mutual benefit democracy, and having tolerance and inclusivity of the rights of lesbian, bisexual, gay, transgender, and queer people created various groups of disgruntled Americans (Love and Tosolt, 2014; West, 2001).

Du Bois fundamentally contends that while blacks have a war within (double consciousness), they can indeed process the Souls of White Folk. Du Bois positions himself within the context of the system's collective record with respect to issues of race and how the exploitation of race yields profit and; therefore, remains tolerable. Du Bois states:

This theory of human culture and its aims has worked itself through warp and woof of our daily thought with a thoroughness that few realize. Everything great, good, efficient, fair and honorable is "white"; everything mean, bad, blundering, cheating and dishonorable is "'yellow'" a bad taste is "brown"; and the devil is "black." The changes of this theme are continually rung in picture and story, in newspaper heading and moving-picture, in sermon and school book, until, of course, the King can do no wrong-a White Man is always right and a Black Man has no rights which a white man is bound to respect. There must come the necessary despisings and hatreds of these savage half-men, this unclean canaille of the world-these dogs of men. All through the world this gospel is preaching. It has its literature, it has its priests, it has its secret propaganda and above all-it pays!. (Du Bois, 1920, p. 461)

Du Bois finds himself thinking deeply about the socialization of race as positioning whites to be omnipotent and the antithesis of which would be black (lesser quality of life). There was a value gap with respect to life between blacks and whites that existed in the early 1900's and this value gap remains a post-modern reality just the same. America continues to be beset by the many manifestations of this daily.

Du Bois states: Slowly but surely white culture is evolving the theory that "darkies" are born beasts of burden for white folk. It were silly to think otherwise, cries the cultured world, with stronger and shriller accord. The supporting arguments grow and twist themselves in the mouths of merchant, scientist, soldier, traveler, writer, and missionary. Darker peoples are dark in mind as well as in body; of dark, uncertain, and imperfect descent, of frailer, a cheaper stuff, they are cowards in the face of mausers and maxims; they have no feelings, aspirations, and loves; they are fools, illogical idiots-"half-devil and half-child." (Du Bois, 1920, p. 460)

This chapter was heavy handed in providing the exact words of Du Bois, with a sprinkle of Douglas, Crummell, Malcolm X, West, Dyson, and Glaude. The purpose was simply to lay out the nuances related to America's race problem from the 1600's up until the early 2000's.

The race problem related to soul appraisals has not been completely resolved with respect to religious and cultural estimations. In fact, this country has not quite rested its case on value of life equitability (Glaude, 2016). What this country has done is bury negative racial appraisals as culturally insignificant and/or perhaps mediated it by successful integration, social mobility, inter-racial coalitions, and responsive policies that foster political concessions. However, the primacy of policing continues to be a cautionary note regarding reverence for black lives. This country is being confronted by evidence of police targeting, profiling, discretion, brutality and lethal force against black bodies. Some see it as necessary policing for a dangerous population. Others compartmentalize it as a problem for a specific class and race of people. Still others protest policing as modern day public lynching and unfortunately, all groups (except for family members) eventually find themselves desensitized or accepting as policing normalcy. As a nation we think we are so far removed from pre-civil rights soul appraisals, nor do we think we are defined by racial ranking theories. Thus, for many this chapter should be archived or dismissed totally. I remain a proponent (as a research scholar and black man) that skin color remains more than a mild curiosity and continues to be significantly related to inter-racial relationships where blacks' contend with tolerable suffering and even death because the souls of white folk are somewhere between not caring, indifferent or silent about the value of a black life.

Du Bois states: A true and worthy ideal frees and uplifts a people, a false ideal imprisons and lowers. Say to men, earnestly and repeatedly: "Honesty is best, knowledge is power, do unto others as you would be done by." Say this and act it and the nation must move toward it, if not to it. But say to a people: "The one virtue is to be white," and the people rush to the inevitable conclusion, "Kill the 'nigger'!" Is not this the record of present America? Is not this its headline progress? Are we not coming more and more, day by day, to making the statement "I am white," the one fundamental tenet of our practical morality? Only when this basic, iron rule is involved is our defense of right nation-wide and prompt. Murder may swagger, theft may rule and prostitution may flourish and the nation gives but spasmodic, intermittent and luke-warm attention. But let the murderer be black or the thief brown or the violator of womanhood have a drop of Negro blood, and the righteousness of the indignation sweeps the world. Nor would this fact make the indignation less justifiable did not we all know that it was blackness that was condemned and not the crime. (Du Bois, 1920, p. 456)

The next chapter examines policing the black body, which is the same as policing the veil. In other words policing the evil nature of blackness. For police officers, they are correct when they suggest that they are doing their job, particularly within the context of their cultural training. The culture of policing may not foster specific language targeting blacks as "illogical idiots, half devil and half child" (Du Bois 1920, p. 460). The culture of policing does in fact include policing populations of people perceived to have elevated propensity, likelihoods or probabilities of engaging in crime (criminality) (Carlson, 2005; Glaude, 2016).

· 4 ·

POLICING BLACK BODIES

Lethal Predatory Habits

Far too many unarmed black males have died at the hands of police officers. This reality warrants exploring how cultural codes influence police officer's perspectives on the black males they encounter. It is not enough to offer another basic explanation concerning instances of black bodies that have been fatally killed by police officers. There have been enough statements professing tragedies and learning experiences, community healing, forging trusts between communities and police officers, and symbolic protests with no real intent to actually engage in a bloody retaliatory revolution. There have been enough social movements galvanized by group energy, only to dissipate when political figures, legal agencies, and media outlets trot out that same old Black Panther Party for Self-Defense attack. The classic accusation being that protest groups that focus on racial proclamations of valued appraisals and demand equitable treatment from agents of the criminal justice system are somehow not genuine, and represent a criminal organization that supports killing police officers. In the same vein, mainstream society quickens their criticisms by suggesting that Americanism should be primary over highlighting the value of black lives as matter of consideration for equitable citizenship.

Are you not tired of listening to lawyers who can't articulate the cultural codes that drive these killings? Where are the lawyers that can secure a conviction? Sure police convictions have been rare. Still the black community needs increased probabilities of convictions to counter notions of police officer impunity. There have been enough civil pay outs that tax payers are footing the bill to finance murderers. Excuse me, noble agents of justice who experienced enough fear to "dead" another black body.

Ask any family member about their lives without their loved ones and the preference would be to turn back the hands of time where their loved one returns home safely. What's more black bodies apparently have no consideration of innocence even if that black body be female (Neely, 2015).

It seems that this country is entertained by police drama that ends the same way, white goodness triumphs over bad blackness. If this country is not entertained, then it appears to be desensitized by black corpses on public display. It has gotten to the point that no other conclusion can be drawn. Whites who are consumed by racial fear accept street executions as opposed to the alternative of encountering black men in undefined places and spaces. The black male body apparently symbolizes unpredictable depravity and the female black body somehow represents an invitation to offend (Anderson, 1990; Carlson, 2005; Glaude, 2016; Neely, 2015).

Black bodies are extinguished with inequitable grief. America proclaims equality before the law for its citizens and yet the practice of due process becomes the process whereby black humanity is negated so much so that it's unidentifiable, leaving no justice for the living and no sanctuary for the dead. Whites outnumber blacks two to one in instances of police use of lethal violence. However, blacks are disproportionately killed by police officers. Blacks are represented in the general population at approximately 13% but make up 20% to 26% of unarmed blacks killed by police officers (Davis and Block, 2018, and Gilbert and Ray, 2016).

They were sons and daughters: Emantic Fitzgerald Bradford, Jemel Roberson, Botham Jean, Terence Crutcher, Philando Castile, Sandra Bland, India Kager, Natasha McKenna, Tanisha Anderson, Yvette Smith, Laquan McDonald, Samuel Du Bose, Darrien Hunt, Michael Brown, Eric Garner, Oscar Grant, Trayvon Martin, Jordan Davis, and Jonathan Ferrell, to name a few.

Scores of blacks have died, enough for a mass grave and there will be more to follow. The sad lesson seems to be that in those instances where white men are in a killing mood, the best defense for black males is to not cross his path. Stated another way, the only guarantee for surviving an encounter with some police officers is to never encounter one. Black bodies can't be too young or too old to have bullets enter their bodies, head shots, torso shots and lethal shots. One wonders about Tamir Rice and what manner of danger he possessed to result in his killing in under three seconds. One wonders about the pending danger a Walter Scott possessed at 50 years old. Walter Scott was shot from behind as he attempted an un-athletic flee from a police officer.

There has to be a script describing the roles that black males must play when encountering a police officer (Anderson, 1990). That script perhaps defines roles and includes complete deference, submission to power dynamics, and sprinkled with some form of hope for the lesser penalty than death.

Anderson details an account where his '82 Delta 88 car was stolen:

> As they exchanged pleasantries, the second policeman kept looking at me with puz-zlement. Black male alone in rear seat. "Oh, somebody stole his car, and we're out looking for it. It's a maroon '82 Delta 88. The other policemen nodded. The two continued to make small talk, but the second officer could not keep his eyes off me. I felt that if I had made a false move he would come after me. In essence the policeman played his role and I played mine: notwithstanding that I was a victim of crime, my color and gender seemed to outweigh other claims. Such roles are expected by the young black men of the neighborhood who have a clear sense of who they are and what they mean to the police. It is from this knowledge that they infer how to act, and how the police will act, believing both must behave according to an elaborate script of the streets. Much of this may be viewed as symbolic display, but it works to maintain a certain ordering of affairs in the public arena." (Anderson, 1990, p. 193)

Conversations seeking clarification from police officers may be viewed as challenges to authority and; therefore, annoying to some officers. Such an en-counter runs the risk of escalating to perceived challenges to authority while simultaneously conjuring fear resulting in the discharge of a firearm.

With this being said, one can kill a black person and be fairly certain; actions will be justified in the court of public opinion, which leaks into the courtroom. Any ingredient of blackness can be victimized and the victimizer can be comfortably certain that his actions will find favor in the eyes of the law, especially if they hold the title of white police officer.

Travon Martin's killer proved that it is possible to walk away from a crime scene that he orchestrated, and then convince a jury that fear guided his be-havior making killing a black teenager a reasonable solution. All of this is pos-sible when shooters are either white or side with whites in America because suffering is reserved for Africans who became black in a country.

Some readers will be turned off by what they have read. So far the content reads far too presumptive and seems generally accusatory towards police. Some will accuse me of harboring prejudiced feelings towards police officers. Some may even suggest that I am implying that all police shootings are unjustified. While still others may suggest that I don't think good police officers exist. This may be where you decide to stop reading. For those, who decide to read further, this chapter will not be a cliché examination of policing the black body.

What this chapter does attempt to do is provide a discussion with predictive value. Meaning, the culture we subscribe to is directly to blame for fatal shootings by police officers. Black masculinity is both interactional and interdependent with society's collective conscience. Hence, black masculinity represents a desperate pursuit to transcend structural, economic, cultural, social limitations, and social forces specific to life course encounters. The life course outcomes of black men across class stratification is dependent upon inter and intra racial value of life estimations and treatment.

Thus, it should be no surprise that black manhood experienced a life course trajectory representative of social status manipulation producing successful assimilationists, fully invested integrationists, operational class ritualists, conformists, rebels, martyrs, criminals, and victims. In other words, the African male who became black in America has experiences on a continuum where on one end are the disposable permanent underclass and on the other end conventionalists connected to the resources and rewards afforded by the democratic money market system. Yet, when thinking about racial casting, it is difficult to remain faithful to notions that mainstream's collective conscience favors positive social capital and affirmations related to black males (Cureton, 2019a; Cureton, 2011). On the contrary, there seems to be a substantial investment in blacks' criminality as the primary ingredient dominating race relations, social regulation, and social control (Eberhardt, Purdie, Goff, and Davies, 2004; Mastro, Lapinski, Kopacz, and Behm-Morawitz, 2009).

Given, police officers are frontline social control agents, they are in the most immediate position to encounter the worst that populations of people have to offer. It should be no surprise that police officers can become jaded with respect to any populations' civil side, especially a black population that has historically been the target for social regulation and control. The primary reason that there is the optics of racially biased police actions towards blacks' is because there has been a history of police brutality and the appearance of racially motivated lethal force so much so that it underscores the race problem in this country. Policing may represent political statements relative to local, state and federal government's racial awareness and disposition. Black communities understand that the government's perspective about them is that they represent a social threat.

Reactive movements (e.g., Civil Rights, Black Nationalists, and Black Power) emerged to address civil entitlements inclusive of black citizenship as deserving of full security, safety and protection from all agents of destruction and demise even if such agency comes in the form of police officers. Social movements, protest groups like the National Association for the Advancement of Colored People (NAACP), Congress of Racial Equality (CORE), and the Southern Christian Leadership Conference (SNCC) emerged; however, their apparent middle class specific integrationist agenda produced college based student groups like the African-American Association (AAA), the Revolutionary Action Movement (RAM), and Soul Students Advisory Council (SSAC). These college groups focused on bettering the conditions and educational freedoms of black students on college campuses but failed to pivot to address the lifestyle needs of grass-roots residents who were far removed from the college scene but experiencing racial oppression just the same (Hilliard and Weise, 2002).

Black Nationalism, Black Muslims and the Nation of Islam was certainly appealing especially when permanent under-class communities were exposed to the aggressive protectionist Fruit of Islam (FOI). However, the religious demands of Black Nationalism as practiced by Black Muslims were too strict paving the way for the Black Power movement, a street version of neighborhood independence, black pride, and black social consciousness. It was through the defiant nature of the Black Power movement that the Black Panther Party for Self-Defense was born (Ture and Hamilton, 1992).

The Black Panther Party for Self-Defense was the street version coalition that policed the police and their actions galvanized police departments to increase neighborhood surveillance with the intent of using lethal force on black men who by nature of being black were threats to social order.

To be black was to be a Black Panther and to be a Black Panther was to be a member of a criminal organization. The top policing agency of the land, the FBI under Hoover's administration empowered police to use brute force to eliminate neighborhood revolts by attacking the Black Panther Party for Self-Defense's operations. The informal directive to restore social order and control of rebellious blacks was to turn the community against the Black Panthers, making them the embedded enemy of the community by: (1) reviving the community's fear of the gun; (2) criminalizing the Black Panthers; (3) disarming the Black Panthers; (4) imprisoning Black Panther members; (5) forcing the community to handle the legal fees associated with arresting and jailing Black Panther members; and (6) destroying the Black Panther's food program, which was thought to be a subversive indoctrination program (Hilliard and Weise, 2002; Hilliard, Zimmerman, and Zimmerman, 2006; Foner, 1970). Needless to say relationships between police officers and lower to working class residents were volatile. With that being said it is appropriate that police departments should subscribe to the fact that policing is a profession that welds them to communities where:

> We are the inheritors of a social history that has been marked by racial and ethnic discord and distrust. Our profession has a duty not to contribute to that discord: instead, we must establish relationships based on trust with all our communities. (Arlington Virginia Police Department, 1999, p. 5)

Policing in America is in fact socially regulating and controlling veils. Policing is extremely difficult because it requires negotiating political minefields, citizen's expectations and racial tensions. The primary veil is located in black communities where they are likely to encounter black bodies who represent some type of criminal.

The problem with this veil is that it promotes black males' master status of being a public enemy, a menace, a troublesome character, deserving of suspicion and in need of inspection to determine socially approved conformity and legitimacy (Anderson 1990). The second veil results from seven realizations that police experience leading to community and policing cohort alienation.

Moreover, policing in America is made more difficult because of the expectation that police officers are problem solvers for the social ills related to community social disorganization, social decline, stratification marginalization, alienation, and racial tension.

When officers are pressed into action they do experience adrenalin rushes, anxiety, anger, and perhaps may be on edge negating complete self-control; however, the immediacy of police encounters does not allow police officers the time to properly compartmentalize their emotions for the reasonable balance that is necessary to perform mistake free policing duties (Carlson, 2005).

> Let's face it: We hire police officers, train them, enthuse them, and then direct them into places that most sensible human beings would never venture, telling them to protect us and keep our streets safe. We ask them to sort through and come to grips with numerous social ills that other authorities in society have long since given up on, and, most often, we ask them to do these things without letting us really see what is required to do so. And there is another very important issue. We ask the police to keep the wheels of our community turning smoothly and to make sure the less desirable members of society are kept at bay but we want them to do it without putting any undue pressure on us personally...officers are obliged to do what they do within

the constraints of the Constitution and Bill of Rights. And therein lies the rub. On the one hand citizens (rightly) demand the police do nothing to jeopardize their (citizens) individual constitutional rights. Navigating that middle ground, the police often find, requires delicate and finely tuned skills. (Carlson, 2005, pp. 1–2)

Policing has to be responsive to political demands and citizen expectations from an organizational standpoint. The bureaucracy must function in a manner that does not violate citizen's rights, and satisfies mayors, governors, and senators' claims about being harsh on crime, and being fair to racially and ethnically diverse communities in a way that accommodates the functionality and welfare of all communities. Yet, the pressure of policing has produced a culture that is more reflective of policing veils, rather than political and citizen's expectations.

The notion of a police culture, though, goes even deeper than the outward symbols that can be observed and measured. In the law enforcement community, culture can be described as an invisible style or a way of doing business that in many ways is more powerful than the rules and regulations of a police department. In reality, it is the unwritten guide to "how we do things around here." The police culture provided meaning and direction to officers and has the effect of shaping, driving, and sustaining the group's choices and actions. It is a force field of energy with an existence and life all its own, and often it is entirely separate from the organizations mission, rewards, systems, policies, and job description. Ultimately, it is the force that controls members' behaviors and attitude in the workplace. And for a law enforcement officer, this can be both good and bad. (Carlson, 2005, p. 29)

Since 2009, the optics of policing has been under heavy scrutiny, which is due in part to social media. Social media and camera phones in particular have become visual records of frontline policing that involves police brutality and the use of lethal force. More importantly, news can no longer be judged by the major networks alone relative to what is considered news worthy, and how to cover a story. Any individual with a camera phone can simply tune in and then post using some arbitrary hashtag that then morphs into a news story.

It is no longer a safe assumption that policing tactics occur in secrecy and can be balanced with police reports. Indeed it is a new era of transparency and pluralistic activism that in many ways have outed police officers. Several police shootings involving the death of unarmed black males have prompted public outcry, forcing news coverage, political attention, and police organizational and committee review.

Police officers are having to contend with stones being thrown at them for doing their job, character assassinations, and adjudicated on some level for criminal behavior and/or civil violations. In spite of all of this, the common outcome is a deceased black person and an exonerated white person. Admittedly, police shootings had been going on long before I became interested. Two cases caught my attention: (1) Tamir Rice; and (2) Oscar Grant, for reasons of Tamir was a boy and Oscar was a father with a daughter. I did watch the original footage of both killings. I do realize the court of public opinion has weighed in and these cases have been processed through the legal and civil system. What is evident is that the value gap between black and white lives was not presented as equal (Glaude, 2016; Neely, 2015). Tamir and Oscar faced double killings, (killing of the body and assassination of character). Tamir and Oscar like so many black males and females were socially degraded to the point of removing each one from public sympathy while simultaneously presenting their over-zealous grim reapers as noble police officers (Neely, 2015). My sociological mind wondered about the core reality of reverence for life while policing the black body.

> Officers have an affirmative duty to use that degree of force necessary to protect human life; however, deadly force is not justified merely to protect property interest. A reverence for the value of human life should always guide officers in considering the use of deadly force. It is in the public interest that law enforcement officers be guided by a policy which the people believe to be fair and appropriate and which creates public confidence in law enforcement agencies and individual officers….The use of deadly force is in all probability the most serious act a law enforcement officer can engage in. It has the most far-reaching consequences for all the parties involved. Thus, it is imperative not only that law enforcement officers act within the boundaries of legal guidelines, ethics, good judgment, and accepted practices, but also that they be prepared by training, leadership, and direction to act wisely whenever using deadly force in the course of their duty. (Broome, 1979, p. V)

Officers are highly trained, highly skilled professionals. However, recall that organizational missions and even classroom learning can be engulfed by the culture of policing. The culture of policing is more reflective of street experiences and prior to that individual experiences throughout one's life course. According to Glaude (2016) racial habits confirm that white lives are more valuable than black lives. Glaude contends that racial habits are more than inferences, but are predispositions, tendencies and vulnerabilities resulting from lived experiences and what we think people are accustomed to and deserve to have happen to them. Racial habits become vulnerabilities to being receptive to stereotypes and biases about black males. Thus, police officers are inherently policing a veil that is associated with representations of blackness as elevated criminality (the potential to do harm). Police officers forged by a lifetime of experiences coupled with policing culture could very well fall victim to cultural codes regarding black males' master status, as criminal. Riding the cultural narrative charts a course to accepting blacks' as differently predisposed towards depravity, making them social health hazards. Police are charged with the duty to protect and serve and often come into contact with people who may not be interested in conformity. Over time there may be a cumulative effect leading police to invest in blacks as having a dangerous disposition. The policing outcome could be making inferences about gestures and intentions as dangerous enough to forfeit rights to life, and; therefore, justified deadly force.

The acceptance of blacks' prevalence/disproportionate representation in crime/prison (population percentage compared to criminogenic representation) continues to fuel the narrative relative to blacks' elevated criminality (the propensity, likelihood, probability of engaging in crime) (Welch, 2007).

Criminality is something to be feared so it is reasonable policing to suppress fear with lethal force. Especially if that fear is shared by white Americans. It is not hard to imagine that whites' fear of blacks' potential to be dangerously violent can serve as a proxy for understanding how police could have the very same fears and make a judgment to use lethal force, independent of visual confirmation of a weapon. The master status of black skin stands alone as a non-verbal threatening gesture where an inference can be quickly made to use lethal force to suppress the ominous threat of death. Anderson contends that black males' master status conjures images of a dangerous street predator, which prohibits him from being considered a law-abiding citizen (Anderson, 1990).

> According to Anderson: on the streets, color coding often works to confuse, race, age, class and gender, incivility, and criminality, and it expresses itself most concretely in the person of the anonymous black male. In doing, their job, the police often become willing parties to this general color-coding of the public environment and related distinctions, particularly those of skin color and gender, come to convey definite meanings. Although such coding may make the work of the police more manageable, it may also fit well with their own presuppositions regarding race and class relations, thus shaping officers' perception of crime "in the city." (Anderson, 1990, p. 190).

Reverence for life is certainly under consideration, only it's the white life that matters. If color can't be stripped then, officers are reduced to thinking, "I am of more value alive to my family than he is to his family." The consequences of lethal force reverberate as a race related shooting because it's hard to separate actions from racial habits and white fear. Moreover it's nearly impossible to dismiss the racial legacy that police officers and blacks share (Carlson, 2005).

> Becker states: Some statuses, in our society as in others override all other statuses and have a certain priority. Race is one of these. Membership in the Negro race, as socially defined, will override most other status considerations in most situations; the fact that one is a physician or middle class or female will not protect one from being treated as a Negro first and any of these other things second. The status of deviant (depending on the kind of deviance) is this kind of master status. One receives the status as a result of breaking a rule and the identification proves to be more important than others. One will be identified as a deviant, before other identifications are made. The question raised: "What kind of a person would break such an important rule?" And the answer given: "One who is different from the rest of us, who cannot or will not act as a moral human being and therefore might break other important rules." The deviant identification becomes the controlling one. Treating a person as though he were generally rather than specifically deviant produces a self-fulfilling prophecy. It sets in motion several mechanisms which conspire to shape the person in the image people have of him. (Becker, 1963, pp. 33–34)

Does this description offered during a time when black people were referred to as Negro, fit modern day cultural narratives? Culture is shared outlooks and cultural scripts (definitions, normative expectations, perspectives, etc.,) that guide behavior. Culture influences our behavior by making us "inclined" to believe, perceive, and act according to socialization. Socialization is significantly related to personality, social and psychological development and directly informs us on how to process and handle situational circumstances (Dyson, 1996; Glaude, 2016; West, 2001; Wilson, 2009). The surviving narrative about black males in particular is that black males have an elevated criminality (propensity, likelihood or probability of engaging in crime and/or un-predictable behavior) (Welch, 2007).

What's more black males possess a difference in soul, spirit and essence that makes his intentions predisposed towards depravity, marking him as a socially dangerous health hazard. It logically follows then that the answer to the question regarding Negro descriptions as applicable to modern day blacks, is yes, because such meanings about the Negro were allowed to survive after civil rights and other race affirmation social movements. Dyson (1996) contends that race continues to matter in all areas of life because of facts, forms, and functions of racism, which ultimately serves as context for interactions (Dyson, 1996, p. 33).

To summarize then police officers contend with policing a racial veil that does not dismiss the impact of racial legacy, particularly cultural meanings that present black males as problematic. Blacks' troublesome potential marks them for police inclinations to used lethal force given: (1) suspect presents an immediate danger to the officer; (2) suspect presents a probable danger to the community; (3) danger is inclusive of movements that permit a policing inference of to not be proactive could mean the suspect has time to kill the officer; and (4) danger is inclusive of attempting to evade police officers, while simultaneously posing a threat to law-abiding citizens.

According to Carlson (2005) police officers cope with seven degrees of veil separation during the course of their careers: (1) special group of protectors, securing functional citizen's safety; (2) officers' placing themselves on a pedestal distancing themselves from others who engage in legal infractions; (3) officers' experiences clearly defines them as special and different from people who are not officers; (4) officer's with longevity and job promotion eventually lose sight of real street level police work that is shared by fellow patrol officers; (5) officers' continued association with peer cohort shift patrol officers translate into the belief that only like circumstanced shift officers understand and perform policing duties; (6) suspicion reduces trust levels to just the officer's partner; and (7) to the degree that partners are perceived as having been influenced by outside social networks, officers further suspect their own partners are acting inconsistently. It appears over time, seven veils are forged standing as wedges alienating officers. These seven veils are dangerous given the pressures of policing (Carlson, 2005, pp. 35–37).

This chapter leads me to conclude: (1) I have a healthy respect for police officers given their general ability to negotiate crime fighting, personhood management, political, organizational, community, cultural and peer group expectations; (2) I could never be a police officer; (3) police officer's split second decisions last a lifetime for the living and reverberate through the community as fuel for protest; (4) police officers live with the consequences of taking a life; (5) police officer's decision to use deadly force does not operate independently of racial habits, embedded in cultural codes; and (6) we have failed one another miserably on both sides of the racial spectrum and policing the black community provides evidence of such failure.

The failure of society to see black men as human will continue to lead to character assaults, and assassinations because black males are not receiving the benefit of the doubt. Blacks' inclusive of black females' victimhood is reduced to speculation of deservedness. Blacks are left with grief, mourning, and stifled potential. The tragedy is that officers' decision to use lethal force on unarmed black men results in killing a minimum of two generations (60 years) of life. Children and children's children will never be born as a result of one lethal killing. Black males going about their routine activities are without security and assurances that one police encounter could result in their demise.

There is anxiety about what should be simple traffic stops or routine exchanges between black citizens and white officers. Speaking from personal experience, there is this elevated dread when peering in the rear view and seeing blue flashing lights. Thoughts crash my reality, *"damn, did I do and say everything I was meant to do and say? Take a deep breath, man. Keep your hands still and visible."* I know all too well that if I die here tonight, I will be without sanctuary.

· 5 ·

PROTEST SPIRIT

Bastardized Activism in Gangsterism

My ethnographic research on South Central, Los Angeles' Hoover Crips revealed that gangs are civil. The revelation that gangs demonstrate civility should not be taken to mean that there was no evidence of troublesome deviance crime and violence. The revelation that gangs can demonstrate civility does not imply that there was no evidence of spiritual deficits. Certainly, efforts at peace were rudely interrupted by passions for killing. Black gangsterism has been overshadowed by the amount of community suffering experienced as a result of gang wars and the Hoover gang has definitely engaged in enough gang wars that has consumed the entire community, which consists of nine street or branches from 43rd to 112th (Cureton, 2008).

> Far too often, gangs are portrayed as detrimental to the community. However, Hoover Crips have a sense of civic responsibility, and have (at times) demonstrated true brotherly love, friendship, and positive guidance. During peaceful times, Hoover transforms into a relatively noble organization that looks out for the best interests of young black males even if it means belittling themselves, and discouraging gang membership. If Original Gangsters think that a young boy has the intelligence, athletic, and/or artistic talent to make it out of the hood, they will do what they can to discourage gang membership. Original Gangsters will socially and financially support such individuals, and negotiate ghetto passes to keep them out of harm's way. (Cureton, 2008, p. 71).

However, civility is overlooked because it does not fit the narrative that gangs are the scourge of permanent underclass communities. To suggest otherwise would be viewed as trampling over the nobility of hard working blacks. The running narrative is that any positive statements about gangs legitimizes their existence. Gangs do not need validation, nor do they seek it from outsiders or individuals or groups that are living the American Dream or have middle class integrationist's agendas. Residents who live in communities dominated by gangs understand one truth and that is that gangs have been around for as long as they can remember.

The existence of gangs is generationally strong and gangs are thoroughly stitched into the social fabric of marginalized settled and un-settled communities (Cureton, 2008).

Dyson (1996) lamented that "juvenocracies" dominate permanent under-class communities. According to Dyson young adult males have considerable socialization agency and wield control over the criminogenic vices in their respective neighborhoods. More than that, neighborhoods with "juvenocracies" are in many respects the parental social control agents, advocates and surrogate normative expectation teachers of the streets they occupy (Dyson, 1996, p. 140). Scholars, in similar fashion to Cornel West, harp on nihilism as the responsive psychological adaptation to strained resources and social isolation. Often equating what appears to be chaotic violence for out of control despair and infinite hopelessness (West, 2001; Wilson, 2009).

My ethnographic research on Hoovers, and my concentration on the history of black gangsterism does not refute the reality of how nihilism has infected permanent underclass communities. What my research does promote is black gangsterism represents means to negotiate respectable manhood and a willingness to survive, and offers opportunities to transcend the limits and restrictions imposed by mainstream and their immediate environment. If blocked access to the American Dream breeds nihilism, then black gangsterism is responsive to blocked access to the American Dream, and has made nihilism a steady part of negotiating masculinity. The major difference is that black gangsterism while on its face seems to produce death, actually offers an investment in negotiating success using a cool pose (Cureton, 2008, 2011; Ladson-Billings, 1995).

My research on black gangs, inclusive of Crips, Bloods, Chicago Gangs and black prison gangs affirms that gangs are extremely dominant, will never completely be eradicated, and will continue to serve as surrogate parents for scores of black youth who turn to the streets to negotiate their identities, secure protection and seize upon social status through participation in whatever underground economy that serves their lifestyle. The major question is, what else is out there that is immediately and consistently available? Promises of a better life through patient, delayed gratification and investment in education is not enough, nor are warnings detailing probable incarceration, victimization and death. Honestly, unfulfilled promises to make the American Dream accessible, wholesale black flight, continued oppressive police encounters and the relentless nature of resource strain has in fact created the type of dominant black gang that has survived every legal, prosecutorial, and formal social control agenda. Additionally, black gangs stand by cautiously and allow peace marches, community assessments, pastors and parents against violence to voice their feelings, only to resume the routine activities associated with gangsterism. Primary to gangsterism is demonstration of black masculinity, seizing control of resources and handling personally defined responsibilities while representing a code of conduct and honor that proves allegiance and loyalty to the surrogate leadership that provided an avenue for success (Cureton, 2008, 2011). Therefore, I confidently continue to endorse the perspective that black gangsterism is both the problem and the solution to the troublesome times in the under-class enclaves.

> The inner city's street history is clear. The street gang (not the family or the church) is the most important social network organization for urban youth. Even though gang involvement has proven to be the surest way to end up a felon, convict, or dead, a significant number of marginalized Black youth continue to gravitate toward gangsterism, whereas older males are finding it difficult to withdraw from the gangster lifestyle. Thus, to become better representatives for the urban underclass and develop a practical blueprint for better living conditions, Black leadership will have to enlist the street expertise of the strongest socialization agent urbanity has to offer, the gang!
>
> Seeking the assistance of gang members, and bringing them in on discussions concerning the needs of the grassroots masses is a risky proposition and one that I'm sure most would denounce as foolish from the start. However, a socially conscious person with some sense of historical understanding of Black gangs might be inclined to agree with me. The gang (in some version) has always been a staple of the Black underclass community. The history of Black gangsterism offers profound evidence concerning how urban poor Black males and incarcerated Black males have handled oppression, isolation, resource strain, deprivation, denial of rights and freedoms, and blocked access to economic and social legitimacy. (Cureton, 2009, pp. 347–348)

Blacks have not had the benefit of full assimilation in terms of enjoying equally, their civil rights. While it is true that racial progress has been slow, racial progress is evident. Significant social movements should be credited for demanding, and securing a society that makes economic, educational, cultural and social mobility possible. The bottom line is that black America is not adrift and bereft of freedom, rights and liberties. However, in pursuing civil rights entitlements, there still remains significant pockets of resistance that intentionally refute notions of human equity on any level. These instances of contested personhood serve as examples that there is a difference in blackness and it is highly likely that most blacks will encounter racial resistance based on racial superiority and/or racial inferiority inferences. Du Bois (1953) noted that assuming that white is central to humanity eases racial integration but more than that accepting even the lowest of handouts from whites must be met with wholesale appreciation. In the instance that there is a hint of dismay coming from blacks then white's true perspective regarding racial superiority and deservedness will surface.

> Du Bois states: So long, then as humble folk, voluble with thanks, receive barrels of old clothes from lordly and generous whites, there is much mental peace and moral satisfaction. But when the black man begins to dispute the white man's title to certain alleged bequests of the Fathers in wage and position, authority, and training, and when his attitude towards charity is sullen anger rather than waste-then the spell is suddenly broken and the philanthropist is ready to believe that Negroes are impudent, that the South is right, and that Japan wants to fight America. After this the descent to Hell is easy. On the pale, white faces which the great billows whirl upward to my tower I see again and again often and still more often a writing of human hatred, a deep passionate hatred, vast by the very vagueness of its expressions. Down through the green waters on the bottom of the world, where men move to and fro, I have seen a man-an educated gentlemen-grow livid with anger because a little, silent, black woman was sitting by herself in a Pullman car. He was a white man. I have seen a great grown man curse a little child, who had wandered into the wrong waiting room searching for its mother. "Here, you damned black." He was white. In Central Park I have seen the upper lip of a quiet, peaceful man curl back in a tigerish snarl of rage because black folk rode by in a motor car. He was a white man. We have seen, you and I, city after city drunk and furious with ungovernable lust of blood, mad with murder, destroying, killing, and cursing, torturing human victims because somebody accused of a crime happened to be of the same color as the mobs of innocent victims and because that color was not white! We have seen—Merciful God!
>
> In these wild days and in the name of Civilization, Justice and Motherhood— what have we not seen, right here in America, of orgy, cruelty, barbarism, and murder done to men and women of Negro descent. (Du Bois, 1920, p. 455)

When I read that passage, I was forced to contemplate whether racial superiority still resonates but remains situationally dormant, as whites accept an easy integration from blacks who submit to (some degree) that value of life gaps are no longer worthy of protest until it hits too close to their turf, their suburban homes, their middle or upper-class lifestyle. Meaning, integrationist blacks are satisfied enough by the resource and material acquisition part of the American Dream. Blacks are content with coexisting, being invited into inter-racial social networks, and demonstrating that they are skilled enough to distance themselves from lower class blacks. That cliché perspective stating blacks are not one monolithic group is code for socioeconomic, cultural, social and status intra-racial ranking.

> Dyson states: Those of us who are integrationists want our cake of mainstream values. But many of us want to buy it from a black baker and eat it in a black restaurant in the black section of town. Others of us want our racial separatism. But we often want it in mixed company: a black dorm at a white university, a black history month in a pre-dominantly white country and a black house in a white suburb. The lure of separatism lingers because integration failed to provide the just society many blacks had hoped would arrive after the civil rights struggles of the '60s. But the failure of separatism is even greater. It has not delivered the *ethnitopia* it promises. The fact is often forgotten when black folk get angry at the slow pace of racial progress. (Dyson, 1996, p. 154)

An alarming number of black people, take some pride in trying to convince mainstream to hold a higher estimation of who they are by intentionally sep-arating from other blacks they think, they are better than. For example, by pushing back on black gangsterism because of the cruelty and havoc they are engaged in shows allegiance to universal Americanism. However, there is a tendency to take it further. Some black people do take that next level step by suggesting that the social conditions while horrible, pales in comparison to the depravity of the people who reside in those communities.

> Malcolm X states: This is still one of the black man's big troubles today. So many of those so-called "upper-class" Negroes are so busy trying to impress on the white man that they are "different from those others" that they can't see they are only helping the white man to keep his low opinion of all Negroes (Malcolm X, in Haley, 1964, p. 117).

Before dismissing this notion, one need only critically think about black flight. Black flight was more than a physical separation from the lower class black community. Black flight involved a complete, economic, educational, social, cultural and spiritual break from the black community. Ultimately, communicating that complete distancing represents being both better off and better than those blacks left behind in under-class communities (Cureton, 2011; West, 2001).

Long forgotten are the trials associated with migration to spaces and places that were dominated by unwelcoming whites who erected neighborhood and social covenants. Long forgotten are the white gangs that had their nefarious recess in black communities, damaging property, victimizing black kids, and attempting to uphold racial travel restrictions. White gangs, were free to invade black communities, in fact they were indirectly encouraged and supported by white authority figures. More than that law enforcement did very little to stand in their way. Long forgotten is the reality of drugs and other criminogenic street vices operating on the fringes of these newly formed black communities (Cureton, 2017; Hagedorn, 2006, 2009). There was very little social order with respect to black communities being the dumping ground for whites' hedonistic pleasures, or organized crime families setting up shop to bleed the black community of its resources and money. Finally, long gone is the memory that black gangs stood in the gap to protest and become active in securing some level of informal social regulation and control that the black adult population would not risk getting involved in. Bastardized activism in gangsterism means that black gangs became the social regulators, controllers and defenders of neighborhoods. These gangs ended white gangs' nefarious recreation of visiting black neighborhoods for blood sport. Black gangs took on organized crime in a manner that forced organized crime families to do business rather than exploit the black community. Some will argue that it is all crime and black gangs deserve no recognition nor should be thought of as activists. Nostalgia about segregated black communities independent of the impact of gangsters, hustlers and/or hoodlums, renaissance men, underground speak easies, and pleasure joints is false. (Cureton, 2008, 2009, 2011; Dyson, 1996; West, 2001; Wilson, 2009).

My time in the Hoover neighborhood was so very valuable. Although I initially began my research on the Hoover gang in 1999, I remain attracted to the South Central community and have established some long term friendships amongst reputable gang members. They seemed caught up in the glory days of gang banging in the 1970's. Speaking about Criping as a gathering of mostly physically fit youth who were very good at fist fighting who would walk to and through rival neighborhoods to test their mantle. Gang banging was far more about competition and reputation building as a fighter more than combative over turf, and drug selling. Gang members were familiar with their rivals and were not particularly focused on killing them. However, the community evolved, spiraling out of attachment with mainstream America becoming further alienated and abandoned due to black flight. Jealousy began to consume black males who then made a hard pivot towards concentrating on controlling a greater share of the onslaught of drugs flowing into the community. The Hoover experience sparked an interest in constructing a community development theory that was more representative of black community development in America as a result of blacks' great migration (Boustan, 2015; Cureton, 2008).

It is estimated that numbers nearing seven million blacks accepted the challenge to improve their respective life course chances by migrating to northern cities because of the promise of jobs, improved wages, and a more representative political and social climate.

Northern cities offered industry jobs that narrowed racial wage gaps, which positioned families to provide better educational opportunities. The south could not compete with the north's labor market opportunities. Southern states experienced a reformulation of sorts as they lost free labor, cash crops decreased in value, and they had lost the ability to control blacks' freedom of movement (Boustan, 2015). In 1895, the south received a white supremacy boost as Plessy versus Ferguson paved the way for segregation and Jim Crow laws. Hence, southern strategies to have a status quo culture of oppression, coupled with agricultural decline, and wage inequality was more reason enough for blacks to engage in their new found existential freedoms and become pioneers of migration. Southern states were losing in upwards of thousands of blacks, which created housing problems for Northern states. More than that the north was not prepared to socially embrace mass amounts of blacks, leading to overcrowding in segregated neighborhoods. This new competition class of blacks were exploited and used as strike breakers against whites who were seeking better wages through job unions. Blacks were viewed as labor market menaces, and destroyers of whites' ability to provide for their families. A continuous pouring in of blacks made whites bitter and they responded by erecting housing and public accommodation barriers and engaged racial intimidation tactics. Ultimately, pioneering blacks would have to contend with whites who attempted to sustain a way of life that they were accustomed to (e.g. living in racially homogenous neighborhoods, and having career employment with respectable wages that supported their families and their kids receiving education in segregated schools).

Blacks' mass migration was about seeking to cash in on the opportunities offered by northern states (the promised-land); however mass migration was contested by bitter whites who tried to apply spook strategies to make blacks uncomfortable enough to isolate themselves and slow migration (Alonso, 1999; Wilkerson, 2010).

The Emergent Gangsterism Perspective describes four stages of community development and also accounts for black gangs' transition from social groups, to protective vanguards, and then ultimately, criminal enterprises. Along the way, scores of young black males were imprisoned, or died during the course of gang banging (Cureton, 2008). During the defined community stage (1920–1929), communities witnessed a racial composition change as southern blacks, migrated north or west in search of employment opportunities and to be free from the south's oppressive conditions. Southern states' attempts to counter blacks' exodus with sharecropping opportunities failed as blacks desired complete separation from plantations by fleeing to smaller less desirable southern places and building communities. A significant number blacks were far too weary of southern culture, places and faces of oppression and left the south altogether preferring to seize upon the rumored opportunities that awaited them in the north and west.

> During community transition: For the most part, the community was based on kinship and friendship associations. Black residents had a genuine commitment to morals, manners, and family. Hence, early black settlements represented cohesive neighborhoods where people were more likely to be intimately connected, and concerned about the social welfare of one another. There was a premium placed on fellowship and worship. Additionally, generational continuity, and unity was valued over wealth, class, and self-conceit. (Cureton, 2008, p. 3).

The mass migration of blacks produced settling communities that were close in proximity to whites, which sparked racial conflict, especially amongst white and black teenagers who were jockeying for turf.

Essentially, white and black families had youth who used the streets to establish racial dominance and although these groups of unsupervised youth were not formally endorsed to negotiate racial restrictions on places and spaces, they engaged in early forms of collective group violence. Both white and black groups were essentially performing their own version of activism where violence was definitely par for the course as each group considered themselves as vanguards protecting their communities and way of life. Inter-racial nearness, coupled with white disapproval and black rebellion provided the conflict necessary for youth groups to transition from neighborhood play groups to gangs (Alonso, 1999; Cureton, 2008; Thrasher, 1927).

During the community conversion stage (1930 to 1965), mass migration was slowed by economic stagnation, which was ushered in by The Great Depression of the 1930's. The Great Depression was a time of decreased wages and ever increasing racial tensions. Jobs and wages had disappeared creating stress for both black and white families (Dobbin, 1993). World War II (1939 to 1945) and the Civil Rights movement (1950 through 1970's) directly impacted economic, political and social systems (Kazuhisa, 2009). The Civil Rights movement afforded social mobility for those blacks who were in a position to take advantage of access to better education, and professional, managerial jobs. The Civil Rights movement provided the opportunity for integration improving the socioeconomic status of a segment of blacks who would engaged in black flight, or assimilation creating a distant middle class and a defined underclass (Kazuhisa, 2009; West, 2001; Wilson, 2009).

> Community Conversion: In essence, the defined community, and community conversion stages produced economically strained, socially isolated, unsettled neighborhoods where young male residents began living by criminal codes of ethics. Residents in these unsettled neighborhoods were exposed to the reality that they were excluded from mainstream society's allotment of opportunities, and resources to achieve financial, material, and social success. Particularly, marginalized male residents did not accept exclusion, so hustling drugs, guns and stolen goods, prostituting women, and gambling became suitable methods to obtain resources, materials, money, power, and social prestige. (Cureton, 2008, p. 4)

During the defined community and community conversion stages the ingredients for black gangsterism experienced a shift. During defined community, youth honored family ties and taking care of their own was a source of racial pride that was made clear by the presence of white youth. White youth groups provided enough of a challenge to define black youth groups as street advocates or vanguards that protected neighborhood turf and also opened up freedom to travel to once restricted places and spaces. Eventually, white youth groups would relent as white families engaged in white flight from neighborhoods deemed too close to black neighborhoods. Ultimately, the white enemy disappeared as the economic, political and social landscape shifted as a result of The Great Depression and the Civil Rights Movement. Defined communities experienced a conversion that included black flight. Adult residents left behind to contend with feelings of abandonment, and an increasing revelation that community resources were becoming scarce created a disgruntled youth movement. Black youth who witnessed the suffering of their parents and now family process and family dynamic dysfunction turned to the very vanguard groups that had proved successful in suppressing inter-racial peer cohort conflict. When communities spiral out of control, lose its attachment to mainstream, and become isolated, with limited resources, these very same communities become vulnerable to drugs and criminogenic opportunities. An underground economy comprised of drugs, prostitution, gambling, hustling, and person-to-person assaults and victimization, calls for a new type of vanguard. The bastardized protest is less about being an activist and more about rebelling against poverty, no matter the course of action. Predatory behaviors took center stage, which is when criminogenic street gangs colonized converted communities.

> Gangster Colonization: Stage three (1966–1989) of the Emergent Gangsterism Perspective was a period when street gangs became the dominant social force in neighborhoods because murder emerged as the definitive measure of respect. In this stage, respect carried a high premium because it represented social currency that governed street interaction and length of survival. As long as the violence remained in the community, it was deemed a local problem, but continued exposure to economic hardships, social rejection, and social injustice led to riots or unrestrained looting, property destruction and personal assaults. (Cureton, 2008, p. 5)

The black criminal gang received no sympathy and was met with inter-racial condemnation and even support for police officers to regulate and control these uncivil agents of destruction before it reaches newly settled black communities, which were again close to white and/or racially mixed communities. Police engaged in heavy handed discipline of persons residing in underclass communities, only policing tactics were deemed as necessary in order to match the violence that was coming from socially disorganized communities. Whites and black integrationists (benefactors of the civil rights movement, the middle class), either supported or were indifferent about police brutality. Ultimately, a new movement that addressed police brutality would emerge to address police brutality. The Black Power Movement, a movement designed to improve economic, political, legal and social conditions of converted communities dominated by gangs did not get the necessary audience or traction it needed until the Black Panther Party for Self-Defense came on the scene in 1966.

> Police brutality against black residents increased seemingly without institutional challenge or proper regulation. Blacks resented police misconduct, and wanted an organization that would monitor police brutality. A significant proportion of South Central's residents were attracted to Bobby Seale and Huey P. Newton's Oakland based Black Panther Party for Self Defense. Established in 1966, Seale and Newton's Black Panther Party was welcomed and appreciated because the organization directly confronted civil inequity, social injustice, and police brutality. The Panthers were a self-defense organization, and stood in defiance of white patriarchal domination, exploitation, and abuse. Black urban youth were also attracted to the Panthers' defiant rhetoric, willful display of guns, and military style. As the Panthers' appeal spread, chapters began springing up in ghettos across the country. The Los Angeles chapter

became strong because it directly recruited youth who were already frustrated, angry, and detached from society. More importantly, these youth were accustomed to using violence to defend themselves. (Cureton, 2008, p. 5)

Chicago and New York had versions of black vanguards, like the Vice Lords and Blood brothers, respectively. The Nation of Islam received attention from lower class residents as well, appealing to notions that a strong black man should be head of household but such a man must be clean of drugs, faithful to his wife, and functional to his community. Vice Lords had a political agenda that included community resurrection, street level social regulation and control that limited police access to black youth. Vice Lords, The Nation of Islam, Malcolm X (an entity unto himself), the emergence of the Black Panther Party for Self-Defense and formidable street gangs were attempting to occupy the minds of black youth and did so successfully between 1965 and 1970. It was during this time that gang violence decreased as youth were focused on community improvement and actively participating in the Black Power Movement.

Vietnam Veterans, who called themselves Blood Brothers were significant to the movement to improve life chances upon returning home from the Vietnam wars. The American front line aggressions of the Vietnam War picked up pace in 1964 and lasted until approximately 1969. During that time black soldiers came to fight with a sense of pride and a need to demonstrate equitable manhood. Blood Brothers united against the discrimination they encountered on the battlefields and the realities of failed promotions. They called themselves Bloods because they chose not to overlook any attempts to belittle their manhood. The unity and camaraderie of Blood Brothers was solidified by the nefarious conditions they encountered on foreign soil (e.g. uncertain life span, the realities of being wounded on the battlefield, horrible images of death, killing of young and old citizens, relative cowards and insecurity of age cohort white soldiers, necrophilia, and the grotesque game of guts and murder for the sake of murder to achieve crazy soldier status).

Blood brothers understood the institutional mandates that they were conditioned to meet under the normative expectations of soldiering. The seeds of discontent on American soil that bred Blood gangsterism is significantly related to the reality that war veteran Bloods dreamed of fighting for a better life filled with the promises of the American dream but ended up coming home to resource, cultural, and social strains, blockages, denials and character assassinations. The final emotional tug was hearing that the war was worthless from civilians who had no clue about the value of the men who lost their lives. Blood Brothers felt used, manipulated and violated. The return to American soil did very little to offset those feelings. Trained soldiers who understood combat tactics and guerilla warfare made a healthy contribution to black American militia groups (Dawley, 1992; Terry, 2006).

Couple the Blood Brothers of Vietnam with Harlem's rumored blood revenge race brothers and the result was moral panic. Malcolm X galvanized black youth when speaking about Harlem's hate gang. Malcolm X would eventually posthumously inspire the formation of the Black Panther party for Self Defense. Harlem had a hate gang scare that caused whites to panic about the potential for retribution. Harlem's Blood Brothers existed in the imagination of mainstream America as a band of young angry Negroes that were organized by Black Muslims who indoctrinated these young males to kill and maim whites. The involvement and training of these black youth by Black Nationalist, created a scare that this Harlem gang was more militant than the average street gang. Even worse, and what essentially brought about the reality of Harlem's Blood Brothers was the endorsement by Malcolm X who believed that militancy against racial oppression represents an intelligent response particularly in those instances where blacks are being murdered by police officers (Breitman, 1965).

> Malcolm X states: I am one person who believes that anything the black man in this country needs to get his freedom right now, that thing should exist. As far as I'm concerned, everybody who has caught the same kind of hell that I have caught is my blood brother. And I have plenty of them. Because all of us have caught the same hell. So the question is, if they don't exist should they exist? Not do they exist, should exist? Do they have a right to exist? And since when must a man deny the existence of his blood brother? It's like denying his family…If we're going to talk about police brutality, it's because police brutality exists. Why does it exist? Because our people in this particular society live in a police state. A black man in America lives in a police state. He doesn't live in any democracy, he lives in a police state…..Any occupied territory is a police state; the police in Harlem, their presence is like occupation forces, like an occupying army. They're not in Harlem to protect us; they're not in Harlem to look out for our welfare; they're in Harlem to protect the interests of the businessmen who don't even live here…And I would be other than a man to stand up and tell you that the Afro-American, the black people who live in these communities and in these conditions, are ready and willing to continue to sit around nonviolently and patiently and peacefully looking for some good will to change the conditions that exist, No!…but we have to live in these places and suffer the type of conditions that exist from officers who lack understanding and who lack any human feeling, or lack any feeling for their fellow human being….I'm not here to apologize for the existence of any blood brothers. I'm not here to minimize the factors that hint toward their existence. I'm here to say that if they don't exist, it a miracle (Malcolm X the Harlem Hate Gang Scare in Breitman, 1965, pp. 66–67).

Harlem's Blood Brothers exist because black people live in a police state with a blueprint designed to oppress. Moreover, Harlem's Blood Brothers exist because blacks don't live in a democracy but a system that exploits, degrades, discriminates, segregates, isolates, and humiliates. Malcolm X goes on to contend that police officers who lack understanding of human feeling, or any feeling for their fellow human being are being encouraged to have the courage to resort to tactics that are inhuman. The results will be terrorist-type tactics as evidenced by oppressed populations in other countries. Anyone who thinks that the younger generation will suffer brutality at the hands of someone just because they are in uniform is misinformed. There is no apology or need to put the public at ease about the existence of a Harlem defense oriented vanguard for if a Blood Brother vanguard does not exist, then policing conditions make such a vanguard necessary (Brietman, 1965).

The Nation of Islam believes in self-sufficiency and a separate state for blacks. The Nation of Islam (NOI) manifesto is an investment in the American Dream through hard work, discipline, virtue, and humility that would be rewarded in a black-dominated economy. The Fruit of Islam (FOI) represented a paramilitary wing of the Nation. FOI enforced the strict rules (e.g., no drugs, prohibited adultery, sleeping during meeting, missing meetings, selling or eating pork, using foul language in front of females, no abuse of females, (particularly members), no weight problems and most importantly meet your quota of selling Muhammad Speaks). Discipline of Muslims often turned violent as violence had become a code of conduct for resolving issues depending on the perceived infraction (Magida, 1996). Unfortunately, Minister Farrakhan and Malcolm X had differing opinions about the fidelity of Elijah Muhammad, which led to Malcolm X's death. Some speculate at the hands the Minister Farrakhan.

> Farrakhan offered: Only those who wish to be led to hell, or to their doom, will follow Malcolm. The die is set, and Malcolm shall not escape, especially, after such evil, foolish talk about his benefactor.Such a man as Malcolm is worthy of death and would have been met with death if it had not been for Muhammad's confidence in Allah for victory over his enemies (Dyson, 1996, pp. 167—via Muhammad Speaks-1964).

The assassination of Malcolm X on February 21, 1965 would reverberate in ways perhaps the Nation of Islam could not forecast. First, it ignited the militia arm of the Black Power Movement, as Huey P. Newton and Bobby Seale were emotionally distraught to learn of Malcolm X's assassination. Malcolm X's death perhaps communicated to gang members that The Nation of Islam was far too religiously restrictive and not following their disciplined lifestyle could mean death. It more than likely communicated to the Black Panther Party for Self-Defense that the Party would be better off concentrating on its own agenda, serving the community and steering clear of the Nation of Islam (Hilliard, Zimmerman, and Zimmerman, 2006; Ture and Hamilton, 1992).

Unfortunately, the turmoil amongst these various vanguards that once captured the imagination of young black men enough to turn them away from deviant, criminal and violent street campaigns became significant enough to be infiltrated, by the Federal Bureau of Investigations. Cointelpro was the vehicle that was effective in destroying the original version of the Black Panther Party for Self-Defense. Cointelpro was also effective in creating a level of distrust between Panthers, The Nation of Islam and black street gangs (Garrow, 1953). Although the Black Panthers would reformulate and The Nation of Islam would continue its course, black gangs restarted their criminogenic and violent campaigns that would ultimately remove them from positive activism (Cureton, 2011; Hilliard and Weise, 2001; Foner, 1970).

> Hoover's objective was to transform the Panthers' political opposition into a movement of criminals and social terrorist that were of no value to mainstream America and black America for that matter. The best way to achieve this goal was to criminalize the Panther's most routine activities, force them into being an economic liability to the community, and engage in a public campaign to discredit their actions and cast them as a negative element that forces police to intrude upon the peace of the community more so than they were already accused of doing. Essentially, under Hoover's FBI administration COINTELPRO condoned tactics (fraud, fudging evidence, deceit, entrapment, discretionary justice, impartial attention, police harassment, profiling, baiting, trumped up legal challenges related to drug trafficking, weapons violations, extortion, narcotics use, and gangsterism) designed to divide, conquer, and weakened what was perceived to be a dangerous black political group. Ultimately, the communities that the Panthers were organized to serve would be the same communities that would expel them.. In the final analysis, democracy rules, the ghetto continues to deteriorate, and have its economic power siphoned away, police continue to openly abuse marginalized populations, and middle class blacks remain at an untouchable distance. What's more maybe the government turned away from its responsibility (yet again) to protect citizens from harm by loosening restrictions that led to flooding the community with criminogenic vices related to a drug economy. The irony now is that the children that the Panther Party proudly served breakfast to are now feeding off of gangsterism and their gangster lifestyle is the only tangible evidence that the Panthers ever existed. (Cureton, 2011, pp. 30–32)

During gangster colonization (1965–1989) activism was the order of the day. There was a level of enthusiasm amongst the youth of those urban areas that had social movements and social movement groups to model themselves after. The focus was on community improvement more than selfish agendas.

The pride was measureable and the youth were purposed and poised to assist, specifically the Black Panther Party for Self-Defense in achieving political recognition, policing regulation, economic independence and self-reliance. All that changed during the final stage of community evolution. During the start of the 1990's gangster politicalization or the complete gravitation towards becoming a gangland consumed the focus of young males. Community activism had run its course replaced by investment in deviant, criminal and violent street codes.

> The fourth stage of the Emergent Gangsterism Perspective is gangster politicalization (1990's). During the 1990's South Central's neighborhoods became socially organized around traditional rites of passage and street protocol. The 90's represented a time when the gang became further embedded in the fabric of the urban, socially disorganized, underclass black community. Each new generation of potential young gang bangers needed a street education to become better gang bangers, so older gangsters assumed the responsibility of passing on knowledge of gangster history, traditional rites of passage, street etiquette, gangster protocol, and hood politics. Street education includes norms concerning survival, territorial claims, gang set configurations and leadership, color coding, hand signs, verbal cues, decisions for gang warfare, and tactical maneuvering, anatomy of drive-bys, gang alliances, truces, and drug distribution. Street education also includes informing young boys about the duties of young cliques, foot soldiers, and little homies, which usually involves deviant, violent, and criminal ways to prove one's desire to represent the gang. Ultimately, the gang offered the promise of unconditional family acceptance, economic and social success, encouragement and support for disciplined violence, and help with the pitfalls associated with living in criminogenic areas. (Cureton, 2008, p. 6).

The modern day black gang has one more activist obligation, and that is taking personal accountability for a youth liberation in their own neighborhoods. It is clear, no immediate assistance is forthcoming from mainstream nor those blacks who are now thoroughly entrenched in their personal versions of the American Dream. The hypnotic effect of gangsterism in its current form of intra-racial, community proximity predation and lethal violence has to be countered by a youth liberation movement that understands that reclaiming black youth from victimization, murderous campaigns and long term incarceration will take patience.

Before a coalition is possible, the gang liberation movement must be spearheaded by gang members who first work out a blueprint for curtailing violence (Williams 2004). Such a movement must include consistent participation and engagement of a coalition of black leaders in government, churches, and universities and members of the black upper and middle class, with first, second, third and fourth generation gang bangers. The critical ingredients for this youth liberation movement are; (1) don't be critical of nor take protest action against the federal, state, and local government because the movement will need the assistance of the government later in the process; (2) involvement of first, second, third, and fourth generation gang bangers and; (3) every available economic, social, cultural and spiritual resource must flow directly into gangland communities (home territory of gangsterism) (Cureton, 2010, p. 47).

The bulk of this chapter is the product of my ethnographic research on the Hoover gang in South Central, Los Angeles. There were participant observation and interviewing opportunities during my tenure as a security/body guard, allowing for more field research on Rollin 20's, Rollin 60's, and Blood gangs in North Carolina. I have been researching black gangs for going on nineteen years using a mixed methods approach that is dominated by ethnography, followed by content analysis. I have also become involved as a gang research expert on several capital murder cases, involving the death penalty. Much of what is offered here highlights my research because I want to make it clear that I see gangsterism as evolving from activism. This chapter should not be taken as presenting black gangs as something noble. What this chapter does represent is my takeaway from doing research on how black males have negotiated their masculinity through gangsterism within the context of the American black experience? I'm not applauding black gangsterism, I am simply recognizing it for what it is.

I recognize that because of ethnographic research, I was inspired to research and decode the authentic realities of life and death in gang dominated neighborhoods. Moreover, I was also interested in the origins and historical life course of gangsterism as a modern day devastating subculture. I have long standing friendships with many gang members and while it matters to me about how they have lived, it also matters to me about how they cope with grief over being incarcerated and/or deal with the constant thought of in-mortality. The Emergent Gangsterism Perspective was conceived out of my direct observations of the Hoover community along with researching community developments and social disorganization of permanent underclass urban enclaves dominated by gangs. I contend that the Emergent Gangsterism Perspective is a model that can logically be applied to any northern or western city that experienced a mass migration of blacks resulting in community transition (Cureton, 2008).

I am not glorifying gangs, gang-life or gangsterism. I have been a witness to their struggles and thought enough of that struggle to continue researching black gangsterism, not only in its current form but also the history of black gangsterism. The demise of many of the gangsters on some level is certain, yet I feel their struggle. Being a black male, I am not completely divested from similar challenges. Essentially, for me then, it is critically important to research their lifestyle to understand the routine activities of gangsterism so that as a researcher I can at least try to explain who they are and what they represent. In closing I offer a final passage about gangster vanguards.

> The sixties was a classic time where revolutionary confrontations existed on a continuum of un-conditional Christian love to passive resistance, civil disobedience through non-violent protests, to nationalistic and black power rhetoric, proactive and reactive grass roots militancy to all out person and property rebellion. In the 1960's and late 1970's the opposition to a black revolution turned fatal claiming the lives of Medgar Evers (6–12-1963), Malcolm X (2–21-1965), Martin Luther King Jr. (4–4-1968), Alprentice "Bunchy" Carter (1–17-1969), Fred Hampton (12–4-1969), and George Jackson (8–21-1971). These formidable men as young as 21 and as old as 39, became martyrs to the charge for racial transcendence. They were demonized, vilified, cast as enemies to democracy, and ultimately put to death. Though I would never personally know these men, they are a part of black history. Had these men lived long enough to age into a seasoned man's life, may be the revolution would have netted wholesale progress instead of a spiraling away from black vanguards to black gangsters. A youth movement can be in step with positive components of a progressive revolution (defined as proactive and reactive steps to improve quality of life independent of government); however, what hampers the pursuit of radical change or racial transcendence is insufficient knowledge of an effective blueprint and/or the forefathers of that blueprint. The absence of true knowledge and a disciplined blueprint more than likely played some part in modern day black gangsterism. (Cureton, 2011, pp. 13–14)

· 6 ·

EDGE RESEARCH

Taking in Ganglands and Violent Scenes

What is relevant about this chapter? Every good record has an A-side (the perceived clean version with cross-over audience appeal) and B-side (the perceived flip-side that contains sketchy content meant for an audience that is receptive to obscenity). The content for *Edge Research: Taking in Ganglands and Violent Scenes* is the B side of ethnography on The Hoover Crips, a South Central Los Angeles street gang and observations from being a bouncer/body guard for seventeen years (dating back to 1999). Much of the information in this chapter contains raw field notes. The notes on nightclubs in Greensboro is at times pornographic. I will present the notes as recorded in my journal staying true to the time sensitive nature and spirit in which the notes were recorded. There are some instances when I will insert extra commentary for the sake of continuity. My notes are provocative, have no sense of political correctness and perhaps will be extraordinarily difficult to digest. The notes no matter the level of obscenity is an attempt to come close to what was witnessed. What was observed was a filthy reality, sickening at times, emotionally hurtful, hateful, sexist, intra-racially judgmental, and borders on prejudice and negative stereotyping. In other words, this chapter represents: (1) field research notes (with lewd adult sexual content at times) on the deviance, crime, violence and sex of different groups of people; (2) family, institution and social realities related to my engaging in edge research; and (3) reflections on the aftermath of having completed research on gangs and the subculture of deviance, crime and violence.

I am a firm believer that the black scholar has a critical responsibility to effectively communicate blacks' lived experiences. The black experience is in desperate need of fresh narratives from a new generation of beautiful minds that have the elaborate conceptual ability to deliver message priorities from our past. This statement is not intended to negate the extraordinary contributions made by an older generation of black scholars. In fact, this book is anchored by their contributions. However, there remains a responsibility, as a black academic and teacher-scholar to explain to the best of my ability the humanity of black people, especially if the black experience is an area of expertise. If I had read something similar to this chapter prior to doing ethnographic research on gangs and the subculture of deviance, crime, violence and sex, I can't say for certain that I would have been interested in pursuing this area of research. In the end the experiences were stressful and the emotional aftermath is forever. What's more after seventeen years of ethnographic research on gangs and the subculture of violence, my colleagues, associates, students, friends, and family who have either come into contact with me while the research was ongoing and/or have read my work looks at me suspiciously. From what I could gather, it was just as difficult for them as it was for me to separate me from the people and situations encountered over years of ethnographic research on gangs and the subculture of deviance, including deviant sex, crime and violence. There are days when I think it was all worth it. Alternatively, there are moments when I wish I didn't observe certain realities because they remain nightmarish. I have published one book, one research article and two book chapters, I would describe as A-side content: (1) *Hoover Crips: When Cripin Becomes a Way of Life* (2008); (2) *Night-Crawlers: The Potential Health Risks Associated with Criminogenic Masculinity and Clubbing* (2011); (3) *Hoovers and Night Crawlers: When Outside In Becomes Inside Out* (2018); and (4) *Introducing Hoover: I'll Ride for You Gangsta* (2002), respectively. That being said with caution and an advisory noted, let's get into the B-side of observations on leisure night clubs and adult entertainment clubs.

> Tucker states: We have seen that the Negro's heritage in America at best has been one of willful neglect at the behest of his white brother. At worst, it has been conscious subjugation by a white community which has stripped him of his manhood, his pride and his incentive by throwing him into the pit of the city and daring, indeed taunting, him to survive amidst squalor, disease, unemployment, depravity. What

little the black man has left when he enters the city's bowels, the ghetto kills off forever. Everything, that is, but vengeance. For the street-corner text books of the inner
city teach the lessons of hatred well, even to the student who refuses to listen. The
depravity, the ugliness, the powerlessness, all combine to make learning easy. Classes
are short-men graduate early. For years, the ghetto's hatred turned in on itself. Blacks
victimized blacks, acting out street-corner dramas in uncontrolled rage, convulsed by
spasms of self-hatred and masochistic feelings, lashing out at innocent brothers for
the sake of conquering someone-anyone-to prove one's existence somehow mattered.
(Tucker, 1968, p. 123)

The Hoover experience has taught me that gangs trap, cripple, incarcer-
ate, kill, and still there is an allure that maintains generational replacement.
Longstanding and entrenched in the social fabric of black communities, residents are dominated by a collection of males and females that have come
together to convert neighborhoods into ganglands. To be a gangster is to be
a super-star, a political prisoner or a martyr and looking at it as simply being
criminal, prisoner, convict or murdered is reserved for outsiders.

My mentor, Charles Tittle once told me back in 1993 that I would not
be able to make a living doing gang research. I took his word on that for a
period of time but eventually would return to do gang research. Perhaps it is
because I appreciate black masculinity and the desire to survive. It is difficult
being a black man in America. I am a product of the ghetto, the projects,
fatherlessness, and a mother who spent my formative years in prison. I was
blessed to make the best of my opportunities; however; I do not profess to be
any better or that much different from the ghetto hustler/the black gangster
that has been demonized.

As, I progressed through my career I approached my mentor again. I expressed to my mentor that I hate the way gangsters have been portrayed and his
response was *"Well Steve, what are you going to do about it? Give it the sociological
attention it deserves."* In a strange way, I wanted his approval and endorsement
to proceed. I did not need it but I am a Charles Tittle sociologist disciple.
Mainstream would have you believe that black gangsterism is a pathological
mode of operation that started in the early 70's and coincides with the underground, black market economy of illegal vices. If this is true, then let's find
that out. I thought one of the most notorious black street gangs in American
history, the Hoover Crips deserved the courtesy of some type of generational
presentation, a legacy revelation through the eyes of the gangster.

Throughout my research, the one constant has been marriage, and then
in 1998, my precious daughter, Nia-Faye was born. My wife, Debbye has been
extremely patient with me, particularly putting up with almost two decades of

moodiness. Sometimes some women have a tendency to press, and/or restrict the movement of men and perhaps eliminate productive endeavors. Debbye was not one of those women. Debbye gave me freedom to go and conduct the research that would take me thousands of miles away in an environment that she like many people held underlying fears about. I never spoke about the dangers associated with my research. Only once have we really talked about how she felt about my work. Our first in-depth conversation about my research, she said, *"it was rough, we had this new child, and you were going off to God only knows where. I knew a long time ago that I had to put you as a person and your trips to LA in God's hands."* I asked *"what I was like when I came back?"*

She responded, *"Well you were always a quiet man but you were a mute for a while, and I did not know how to take that. I wanted to ask what happened but I never did. I just waited and you eventually came back to us."* I never knew that I came across that way. Therefore, it is important to figure yourself out as much as you can before you engage in ethnographic research on deviance, crime and violence.

Honestly, I had a death wish. Where could I go where men grow up fast and are hardened by life course experiences? If I survived, I would win freedom, a consciousness of kind, and I could return home a better man. In a way, Hoover offered me something that was missing, a look at other fatherless men and how they were surviving. I am not afraid to die. I am afraid of living a life of meaninglessness. My desire is to please God and be mindful that my imperfections should not get in the way of trying to get it right the next time. My deepest ambition is to love and be a good father. I pray that my God, grant me enough time to love deep into energy, be a good father, and contribute something of value that is useful for intellectual currency.

While in the field, many gang members asked *"what kind of a researcher are you?"* I suspect they were suspicious as to whether I was there to investigate crimes or to understand their lifestyle. Researchers doing ethnographic research on gangs had better settle this matter as quickly as possible or be prepared to deal with the consequences of a misunderstanding. Moreover, my advice would be to train your body for the pressure and the stress. Gangsterism is a physical thing and Crips appreciate that hard edge look that a muscular physique communicates. I had that once upon a time because I trained for it. Condition your mind for the possibility and or potential of the interplay between participant-observation.

For those students thinking about doing ethnographic research on gangs there are a series of questions that are necessary to think about and have answers to prior to entering the field. How are you going to handle those thousand yard stares? The kind that looks for weaknesses to exploit. How are you going to handle the moments where personal challenges are thrown on the table and you don't want to hide or defer to the shot callers you are with? How are you going to handle, tests with pit-bulls, those I will be right back, wait in the car times, those bone out or get ghost (means run) moments? How are you going to handle the heat, the smell, and the blood? Are you prepared to get down? On one occasion, I was told to "shut the fuck up" and without hesitation I replied, "fuck you," turned the camera off and took an aggressive stance. I had made up my mind instantly that I was going to give it to him (fight to win) or he was going to give it to me. It did not go down. The gang-sters I was interviewing calmed this dude down because he was interrupting their interview. Mann (a Hoover gang member himself and my primary guide through Hoover) was there. He simply said *"Dog, I know you a man, you got to show respect until they show you something different, so you did the right thing."* When word got back to Duck (an Eleven Deuce Hoover Crip), he immedi-ately wanted to handle the situation. Duck and I have attached to one an-other and we are like brothers often signing off with "peace, love, loyalty and respect." Some days, Duck is Tyrone and I am Brother Steve. On other days, Duck is Duck and I am Cool Breeze (a street moniker he assigned to me). To this day, this gangster's identity that told me to "shut the fuck up" has been kept a secret from Duck to prevent retaliation.

Every researcher has to understand the environment you are entering and what is the potential that you may wrestle with morals, ethics and what would be considered crossing the line? Researchers need to have a thorough understanding of your recording equipment. What is the difference between advertised battery life and field battery-life. Nothing is as good as advertised or perhaps there were times when I simply forgot to turn off the camera. The les-son learned is that there should always be a back-up battery or power source. Understand that the camera is your "eye." Trust me there will be events that will force you to forget taping because you want to see with the "naked eye" and when you do this, you lose valuable data. Keep your eye on the lens.

The Hoover research started in May of 1999, when I spent 14 days in the Hoover community with gang members. I then returned in August of 2000 to spend 10 more days, for a total of 170 day and night time observation and interview hours (Cureton, 2008). The critical question from ethnographic purist centers on the question, "Is 24 days, 170 hours enough to qualify this project as ethnographic research?" The job of the ethnographer is to arrive at some understanding of a phenomenon by sharing on some level in those experiences. The length of time is debatable; however, I felt I fulfilled my duty as a social scientist by emerging from the field with some understanding about cultural codes and quality of life for gang members in one South Central neighborhood (Cureton, 2008). Another research note is that there is a psychological difference in time, which is contingent upon the volatility of a situation (Daynes and Williams, 2018; Feldman and Aldrich, 2005; Finklestein, 2005; Ocejo, 2013).

Those who have experience in the field know that the time spent in the field is not comparable to conventional time. In other words, 24 days or 170 hours seems like very little time from a conventional standpoint, but when you are in an environment where gang wars are ongoing, there is a significant difference in time. I leave you with a story, similar to the traffic light situation presented in the preface. One five minute experience on Hoover is not the same as five minutes sitting in the safety of my campus office. It is about 10:00 at night, and Mann and I are driving through the Hoover neighborhood. As we neared our destination, Mann had to be careful to avoid streets designated as war zones. We heard the sounds of gun fire bursting through the otherwise silent night. I was scheduled for an interview at 10:30, but we arrived five minutes early. Mann stopped the car in front of a house. No one appeared to be home, Mann turned to me and said, "I need to go up here, and check on the Home boy, to see if he is home, and ready to talk, so you stay here." Mann pulled slightly over in the street, only allowing enough room for other cars to maneuver by. He exited the vehicle, leaving it idling. I watched him disappear into the darkness. I could not make out what was happening on the porch because there were no lights on. I saw the door open, and Mann went inside, shutting the door behind him. Here I am sitting in this car, listening to sporadic gun fire. I turned the radio down, and scanned the area. I sat there for about two minutes. I contemplated getting out of the vehicle, and going up to the house, but how would that be perceived? I would look like a coward. Another minute goes by, and I see another car approaching. The vehicle slowly advanced towards the car I am sitting in. Once parallel, the other vehicle stopped. I kept my head straight, but shifted my eyes to the left (where the occupied vehicle was) to better focus on the situation. The window rolled down, and I saw two males. The dark backdrop, heavy base tone grounding the violent musical lyrics, smoke coming from the vehicle, followed by the scent of "the chronic" (marijuana), contributed to a sinister aura. My ears tuned into "shick, shick," the distinct sound of a bullet being positioned in the chamber of a firearm. The sound was not crisp enough to be a small caliber firearm. The sound was heavy as if a bullet with more potential for damage was being loaded. Never turning my head, and hoping that I had imagined that sound, I sat motionless. "Fuck, is this really happening?" My hand automatically reached for the door handle, but I knew if I opened the door, the overhead light would illuminate the vehicle enough to provide a clear target! "Lord let this be my imagination, and if not, make them miss" then as slowly as the car had approached, it drove away. I looked over my shoulder until the car was out of sight. I was out of my mind with discomfort. I decided at that point to lower the passenger seat, so that no one could see me. I lifted my head, many times in an effort to remain aware of my surroundings. Suddenly, out of nowhere, Mann appeared. He jumped in the car, noticed the reclined passenger seat and asked, "What you doing?" I replied, "Taking a nap." I hid my concern, although I don't know how well because Mann just laughed. Before I finished thanking the Lord (in the privacy of my mental thoughts), Mann informed me that my subject was ready to be interviewed. I looked at my watch, and noticed that it was just 10:30, which meant that only five minutes had elapsed. What's more, the subject to be interviewed was Chim. The 24 days or 170 hours of field time in one neighborhood in South Central was intense. The seconds felt like minutes, the minutes like hours, and the hours like days. (Cureton, 2008, pp. 94–96)

The aftermath of my research on the Hoover gang has been a combination of confusion, concern, and negative inferencing. Certainly, the various institutions that I am associated with indirectly dictated how much disclosure could take place without jeopardizing comfort levels. I know that had I written about everything, it would have intensified the aura of suspicion that continues to surround me.

Quite frankly, there is a degree of separation between me and other faculty members at the University of North Carolina-Greensboro. There is a void, a space of "unknown." What would that unknown manifest as if they knew more? I know that I am an aggressive black man and I know that my masculinity dial is set on 5 when in the sociology department and on campus, thus my image is softened a great deal. However, on Hoover I got a chance to turn it up to 10! Once again being free! What ya'll know about Cripin,' Hoover Dust, block to block, the wind and the sun, the ground, the night-time air, blow ups, pipes, LO's (left overs), and cobra backs? On the west coast the saying does not go "what's crakin," it's "what's happenin," a statement usually clarifying what level of violence is about to occur. What you know about free fire zones and being there for the homeboy, no matter what? What you know about finding packages and rolling in enemy territory to give it back? What you know about riding shot gun, prepared to fire on command, understanding if you drop someone, you charge it to the game? What you know about masking and being entrusted to be the rider? I never wrote in detail about certain observational experiences because it is best to take somethings to the grave. Confusion blurs ethical lines.

In the book *Cripin on Hoover: When Cripin' Becomes a Way of Life*, there is a traffic light incident that appeared to be escalating. I made up my mind to be with Hoover and what's more, I wished I had a gun. How many times, have I been asked did I really mean that? As popular professional wrestler Stone Cold Steve Austin would say, *"Can I get a hell yeah!"* Just the mention of an honest hiccup of desiring a firearm for safety and security, alarmed some of my colleagues.

> Time seemed to vary with each situation, which produced psychological differences in the length of one minute. For example, from a conventional stance, traffic lights have a standard time, some longer than others, but still there is a time, and of course, time does not stand still. On the third day of my initial visit to South Central, I had just finished some work out at Manchester Park (a recreational park in Hoover territory). Mann, from Five Deuce Hoover, Duck, from Eleven Deuce Hoover, and I were leaving, but a red traffic light at a small intersection halted the vehicle. From the passenger's side of the vehicle, I noticed four black males standing by some pay phones on a corner less than 10 yards from the car, but I did not think anything of it. I kept my head straight because in the hood you don't stare unless you are prepared to deal with the consequences of staring. Duck notices these same black males, but there is something he does not like about them. Duck (sitting in the back seat of the vehicle) starts yelling out the window; "I hate these drug dealing niggas. Look at that shit! Mann! You see that! Yo! What's up nigga? Duck! from Eleven Deuce, nigga! What ya'll want? Yeah, that's right!" He represents Eleven Deuce Hoover by flashing Hoover gangster hand signs. Mann from Five Deuce Hoover, starts laughing as he says to me, "see, told you Duck be tripping sometimes, I told you he is a real gangster." Those black males peered into the car as Duck kept representing. By this time the situation appeared to be escalating, and Duck was clearly the aggressor. My heart started racing as my mind kept spewing thoughts like "damn, it's about to go down, right here, right now, and why the fuck is this light still red?" I looked down between my legs, and noticed my camera and note pad, but my mind was thinking, "shit, I really need a gun." My heart was racing as my mind had to remind me to breathe. Instinct took over as I immediately turned my head to look at these brothers, who at that very moment became enemies to my survival. I looked at them thinking, "not to-fucking day; whatever, I'm with these niggas, right here." The mutual exchange of looks was enough to gang affiliate me. Those brothers never said a word; they just stared at the car. The light turned green, and we drove away. How long was that light? I venture to say possibly thirty seconds to a minute, still no more than sixty seconds in it, right? Even a 30 second light can feel like an eternity or enough time to sweat, develop a dry throat, and become filled with energy. That traffic light lasted just long enough to allow for a potential confrontation to develop. I felt that if anything were to go down, I was going to have to get involved whether I wanted to or not. That traffic light incident instilled in me the understanding that time is relative, and that one minute in the hood could be the difference between life and death. The traffic light incident underscored the fact that the Hoover gangland represented a different social setting. (Cureton, 2008, pp. IX–X)

Two loyalties were called into question regarding the Hoover research: (1) first, the so called black intellectuals were upset because my research exposed private conversations about the true nature of black flight and how gang members have actually processed the fact that they know certain blacks don't care about their existence; and (2) second, my beloved membership with Omega Psi Phi, while never in jeopardy, did strain relationships as the fraternity did not appreciate being associated, affiliated or compared in any manner to a street gang (Cureton, 2009, 2011). After publications about Hoovers and the legacy of black gangsterism, I think I managed to provide a good account of residency on Hoover. I got close enough to get authentic disclosures from people (e.g., mothers who lost sons, preachers, true blue gangsters and residents who are simply tired of living in a gangland) who live on Hoover and I did it by going to South Central. The Hoover book has been out since 2008, and has circulated through the Hoover community and has exchanged hands in penitentiaries.

The book certainly has its critics. The primary irritation, is that the youth of Hoover don't appreciate being called Crips because they are pushing Hoover Criminals or just Hoovers, while others are restricting to a smaller Set gang. There have been opportunities to return to South Central to write books on other gangs, specifically other branches of Crips and Bloods. I have declined to do so because I am still recovering from the Hoover experience and the ethnographic research on the subculture of deviance, crime, and violence in North Carolina.

Does North Carolina have the potential to become a gangland? North Carolina is beset by crews, cliques, posses, near groups and transplant gang bangers who can unite and recruit gang members. The latter part of 2007 witnessed so much attention on the gang problem in North Carolina.

I was asked several times to give public lectures, television and news-paper interviews. I was even asked by the New York Times to give an account. I refused because I did not want to add to the moral panic. I understand how the media works, so instead I lectured students using a content analysis of newspaper articles spanning a decade (Greensboro News and Record) to demonstrate how what was being said in 2007, was said in late 1990's.

The following is a sociological summary of ethnographic research on the Hoover gang. One lesson learned was that the gang is a product of the "farmer's harvest." Meaning the gang represents a manifestation of social, political, economic, structural, cultural and spiritual shifts in the black community. More specifically, the Emergent Gangsterism Perspective (EGP, 1920–2009 and beyond) suggests that the context of gangsterism is; defined community, community conversion, gangster colonization, and gangster politicalization. The EGP perspective suggests that blacks have a unique history of generational humanistic deprivation that has contributed to the decline of the black community and the formation of black gangs. Gang membership causes criminal behavior and attracts boys who are already criminal. The fresh element here is that gang recruitment seems obsolete. Moreover, in an economic and resource strained, isolated environment, the secular salvation (respectable survival and dignified death) offered by Hoover is fundamentally essential. The perceived need for this "secular salvation" is enough of an attraction to make the need to recruit un-necessary (Cureton, 2008).

Research has shown that in a male dominated gangster environment, male gang members, more than female gang members participate in the seriously violent crimes. Gangster females' involvement in such crimes was relegated to "auxiliary" (weapon carriers and/or drivers) or in a significant number of cases, total exclusion. Even though, this project was focused more on masculinity in the gang, issues concerning perceptions of female gang members did come up. The normative expectation that female gang members are excused from participating in all aspects of gang banging, including murder or that females should not be "targeted for murder" is not relevant for Hoover (Cureton, 2008). The data reveal that female gang members are expected to do the same things as male gang members.

Another significant finding is that in a seemingly chaotic environment, "ghetto passes" (informal control mechanism that governs safety and affords protection for designated individuals) imply that inter gang relations are governed by street protocol. Hoover does have compassion and at times, demonstrates true friendship and civility. According to Mann, from Five Deuce Hoover, the gang will shun athletes, and others deemed worthy of something better than a life of gang banging, away from the gang. This suggests that gangs have a sense of reasoned responsibility and recognize what it takes to be successful in mainstream society.

Moreover, it appears that some older gang members have a better understanding of the impact of long term gang banging, inclusive of incarceration and trying to regroup or gain traction in the conventional world after having served time. Furthermore, gang banging requires that those who go on missions don't second guess their obligations to the gang, which is quite possible if a gang banger has hopes of being successful in the conventional world. This would mean that hope could be used as leverage to acquire cooperation with police officers in helping solve crimes and/or get other gang members arrested.

Chapter 3 of the Hoover book details the nuances of peace and war. There is an aura of "living in the shadow of death." This chapter, has been described as off putting for those who don't necessarily align themselves with Christianity. This was the chapter that convinced my critics that I was not an objective researcher.

For these critics, openly admitting to the power of God, and the spiritual element introduced in this chapter is subjectively emotional and thereby possibly elusive enough to prohibit sociological measuring. On a more secular level, the gang has proven to be a steady force to offset the perils of social disorganization, social decline, and strained resources, blocked socially approved legitimate opportunities for success, as well as numerous other status inhibitors, criminogenic opportunities, dysfunctional family dynamics, collective predation, and individual behavioral volatility. The gang situation remains in this state (Cureton, 2008).

Ethnography specific to the subculture of violence has a shady side. For the past fifteen years (2001–2016) I have been thoroughly embedded in the local night club scene by way of being a bouncer/body guard. I started withdrawing from the field towards the end of 2016, a process that lasted throughout 2017.

The thoroughly embedded approach included a heavy dose of participant observation. Since, completing the research on Greensboro, North Carolina's nightclub scene, I have at times contemplated whether I was a professor who became a bouncer or a bouncer who became a professor. It would seem that the two exist on opposite sides of the continuum. However, the roles ran parallel and intersected at times making it hard to determine the role that was appropriate for the situation.

There are participant observation nuances related to researching deviant, criminal and violent subcultures, groups and/or gangs. Being black provides a degree of privileged access to certain populations, subcultures and behaviors. Moreover, the findings can be compartmentalized, scrubbed for offensive content, or cautiously trotted out so as to not be offensive, or become evidence for deficient moral character.

Black researchers can encounter some level of hesitation in presenting what was observed with respect to deviance, crime and violence. The B-side content relative Greensboro's nigh life environment represents an un-edited presentation of the notes, infused with my emotions at the time that the events occurred. I am stepping aside from the role as a protectionist cultural gate-keeper (Sawyer, 1973; Washington, 2006).

Sifting through my journal entries revealed two dominant questions; (1) what's happening to me; and (2) what has happened to me? If you let the so called "bout to boys" (boys that always claim they are about to do something to you) tell the story, I am supposed to be dead five times over. For that is the number of times that I have had my life threatened. The first time I was threatened, I heard the words "*I am going to kill you nigga.*" The second time I heard "*you ain't gonna make it home tonight.*" The third time, I heard, "*this is the last night you are gonna breathe.*" The fourth time, it was said to me "*you are gonna die tonight.*" The final time I was told "*I will be fucked up and leaked to death.*" When I heard my life being threatened and mentally processed these threats as credible, I moved to suppress the source of the threat. My rational at that time was to dismantle their over-hyped masculine fronts. The most chaotic of times, I have sat on my front porch thanking my God for another blessing of returning home un-harmed. Other times, I have sat on the front porch gazing at the stars and wondering when police officers would arrive to ask for identification, and inform me that my behavior warranted an arrest. During those times, the stars seemed to shine the brightest when I thought my freedom would be compromised by an imminent arrest. Fortunately for me, my actions were fully supported by club owners and promoters. At the end of every night, my performance as security personnel was evaluated and even though I knew how much support I had, my mind continued to play tricks on me.

My personal worries about being arrested started to fade and the applause and pseudo fame of being someone not to play games with took center stage. I admit, I liked that reputation. There were so many physical confrontations. I had tasted my own blood and I had caused others to bleed and although I still believe that I was acting out of self-defense, I feel a small degree of remorse for engaging in those physical confrontations. Don't get me wrong there was certainly pride in knowing I had defended myself well. In response to the first question, "what's happening to me?" My honest assessment is I was made to meet violence with a rage of my own and so proved myself worthy enough to continue to be considered a top tier bouncer. In response to the second question, "what has happened to me?" I would have to argue that hindsight forces me to acknowledge that my aggressive responses were probably foolish. Regardless, I have learned more about who I am and often times my role of professor by day and bouncer by night made it difficult to be mindful that this was all about ethnographic research.

The last physical altercation I was involved in (August 2015) was so unnecessary. I anticipated this guy would be a problem 3 months prior to the altercation. I made it a point to speak to him one on one to clear up any personal issues that I felt was effecting his disrespectful actions towards me. I thought we had come to an agreement to be mutually respectful, until we found ourselves in the presence of people we both felt would be responsive to aggressive impression management. Still, I warned him, which had no effect so damage was quickly done to him. The police were on the scene, shortly after and ruled it self-defense because he had a gun. I regret the situation but I don't regret it happened to him. Some people keep messing with you until you give them a definitive response in a violent language that is understood.

The most outstanding emotional moment is hands down the murder of a young lady. After about nine years of witnessing violence, you come to expect it and are actually desensitized when it happens; however, there is always one that I have never been able to get over. It was a senseless murder. My thought at the time was *"Greensboro is filled with people who need killing, this one was not one of them."* It's a freezing Saturday night but the transition into an early Sunday morning would prove to be a tragedy. When I first noticed her in Club Plush about 1:45 a.m. November 28, 2010, my first thought was why was she here? She was too beautiful, too spirited, and too full of life to be in a club frequented by drug-hustlers, street-thugs, and gangsters. Her name was Bria and every club security working that night was aware of her presence. She would be murdered less than 45 minutes later. She was shot by bullets leaving a gun barrel nameless but finding her. It broke my spirit. As I stood there and witnessed that "young black beautiful girl" lay motionless, having no resistance to forced motions of emergency personnel and police officers, my inclination was to run over and breathe life back into her. Dre (the club's inside security) is standing next to me saying *"this is fucked up, this is terrible, how the fuck they going to get away with these Sheriffs out here?"* Shaun (another one of the club's inside security) says *"it don't look good, man she not going to make it, some father somewhere is going to get a call that will rock his world, man I got two little girls, how did the shooter get away?"* I realized no one had any answers, let alone the power to revive her. My immediate emotion was disappointment in God for not showing up like I wanted Him to show up. Standing there, reduced to a simple spectator, I prayed, *"my God do not allow this don't let her slip away, do something, please."* The faithful Christian may offer that what God did was call her "home." The faithful Christian may offer that God claimed her on this night to give her the gift of eternal life.

As for me standing there that night, looking at the scene, there was nothing other than the helpless thought of being powerless before the energy of death. Rest in peace sweet angel, and God bless the family. I have revisited the club, sitting on top of the hill and just thought about that beautiful young lady. Club Plush has since been demolished. My notes have it, the shooters were able to get away because the Sheriffs on duty were black and far too interested in what the women looked like inside the club. They were out of position, period. We needed those white Sheriffs, those guys played no games and were on point. Unfortunately they were not working that night.

I was in search of the night-time realities that can't be explained away by the dawn of the day. It is imperative to again mention that the following reflects field notes taken when I was not in the most professional mood. The notes are B-side in content; and therefore, not edited for appeal. I was a thrill seeker and wanted to do research that came close to the adrenalin rush, I experienced on Hoover.

The money is good, could be better but it was cash at the end of every shift. I approached Rock, head of Protective Services, Guns for Hire. *"Rock! let me in the game, shit I damn sure got some Guns for Hire"* but he did not see the fire and told me I was not ready. I am thinking all along, I'm more than ready, ready, as ready could be, I'm tipsy on frustration and anger, got to let some steam off but if the situation is right, I will keep it steady. *"Rock, let me in the game man, put me in the game, I just want to be a player not a coach."* Rock said *"Alright, Bruh, you start at the Klick, where the niggas come like roaches. You better be prepared to watch their every move, including their deceiving approach. And the drama that they bring is sure enough guaranteed, are you ready to get down or what?"* My response was *"shit Dog, let's get down, ain't no or what.*

Violence, I don't give a fuck, I want some of that money truth be told because that Ph.D. is the Dr. Jeckill but this violence shit is my Mr. Hyde. I'm into to that cash if you dig, so pay a brother for protecting and securing shit." Hell that Ph.D. feeds the family and pays the bills but what's wrong with adding in a little something to make it better, you know better is good but "mo better" is great. Did I mention cash in hand at the end of the night just to stop a fight? There is nothing like a hand shake with cash greasing that palm before the shake is complete. Cash means more meat at the table. The more meat at the table, the more I get to eat. We talking about night-crawling, not day crawling and that fool Dr. Cureton is not in charge at night. The alter ego Mr. Hyde, Mr. Aggressive, Mr. Showtime, Mr. You need Anger Management, Mr. Don't make me fuck up somebody is in charge. I'm not bad but I am not scared. Call me Mr. Security, my job is to intervene when the black people hit those demonic switches and turn into niggas and bitches or when the white people turn into whatever it is they turn into when they do that weird ass party yelling, face sucking, drunken slumping, body to body bumping and pumping. Damn are you all dancing to the beat or the words? Just curious, I mean really. When they get to fighting we got to break them off too. Violence does not discriminate.

My first taste of violence was in 2002. I am on my first hunt at the Klick. The spot is a hole in the wall off of highway 29. All the thugs and thugettes are there. Mobb Deep should be coming through and my job is to secure the stage. The Klick is an 18 and up spot so you have underage drinking, smoking, sex, you name it. It reeks of sex in here. These people are un-disciplined in their hedonism, having sex on the dance floor. When the crowd clears, the evidence is in the used condoms on the floor.

Mobb Deep comes through about 3:00 o'clock in the morning. Hell they are late and the natives are restless. These two little dudes, can't be more than 5'2. They moved the angry crowd with three good rap songs, got the money and bounced! During their performance I thought I was going to have to deal with female fans but the females could not get near the stage because the males were fighting to get on the stage with these little midget rappers! Everybody wants to be seen, get discovered, and prove how hard they are.

Every dude I tossed off the stage kept coming back. Hell these dudes ain't just roaches, they cock roaches! Needless to say, I made it through that night, broke up some fights. The Klick had it going on, alcohol, drugs, music, naked females, straight-up sure enough dry humping and grinding that makes Dirty Dancing look like an animated Disney movie. All the brawling you could handle. Whatever is in the music, take it out because it seems to make these people want to have sex or fight. I prefer to let them find them a girl and do whatever is mutual, and get the hell out.

The Defining moment has arrived! Oh Man, it's on! The D.J. blurts out "SECURITY" We are too late. Security fifteen deep and that is still not enough but we came ready to rock. You ever heard the sound of fists pounding on flesh. It's almost like muffled claps. The crisper sounds suggest a targeted connection, the kind that makes faces swell. Mouths are bloody, eyes are being closed, faces being swollen. Fists, and bottles flying everywhere. Those not wanting involvement are running out of the club. It's my first grab. I grab some dude and shove him out of the club, directly on my heels are other security with other combatants. Even more rush out behind them to the slogans of "south side, and Tre Four." Outside security immediately starts spraying everybody.

That pepper spray is no joke. It burns and chokes. Many fall to the ground, yet for others, it's like spraying a dollar can of roach spray on a king cock roach so they keep fighting. Hitting everybody that they don't recognize. You know what is next? Gun Shots! PAC, PAC, that is the sound with a meaning of everybody better get low! Oh, somebody shot inside the club! Another slug comes crashing through the window, announcing bad intentions! We are blessed this day, and no security is shot.

My transformation was noticeable to some veteran security guys. A few will tell you that when I first started, I was not aggressive. I was not into yelling and pushing an intimidating aura on people. I was the one asking for cooperation. Sir could you please do this or that? Or Sweet heart could you do this or that? Please this, please that and a thank you in the end. Well after working a Carolina Theatre party, Doom (one of the lead guys) slapped my pay in my hand and said in front of the entire team *"Steve you are going to have to be more aggressive."* That was humiliating to me. Honestly, I was pissed. *Okay, "motherfuckers" if that is what you want, I can give it to you.*

As more and more fights broke out, I just started not caring as much and started grabbing people with little regard for them. I was perceived as cool to work with by then but still I had not gone off on anyone so I was still "suspect." On another occasion a fight broke out between the Omegas and the Aggie Football Players. I realized, I was too small to handle the big jobs and I hated that feeling. Then on another occasion, I jumped on the back of a guy and he just gave me a piggy back ride on his way to get at his target. The security team said I just grabbed him wrong and that could happen to anybody but again I felt too small or not strong enough. I vowed to never let that happen again, to feel like another man's book bag.

I hit the weight-room as if I were 20 and trying to go to the league (The NFL). I did it with intensity and along with it came a more aggressive style of management. No more *"please do this or that."* It's more like *"homie get your ass in line, do this or get the fuck on."* *"Listen chick, fuck all the mouth you giving, we ain't trying to hear that shit, do this or take your nasty ass home."*

I was working one night at a white club downtown called Greene Street. They started playing that "aggressive zone music" you know the kind that makes black men think they the hardest that ever lived. Anyway this young dude was acting up too much. When I went to talk to him. I blurted out, *"calm the fuck down or get the fuck out!"* He replied *"I ain't going out for nothing."* I thought he also spit on my hat. Well, I lost it!! I said *"motherfucker, I'm going to kill you"* and proceeded to do it. I snatched him up, attempting to choke the life out of him. Security was on me like I was one of the offenders. Truth be told, I was acting wild. I rushed him from the middle of the floor to outside and threw him not realizing another security caught him. Still in a rage, all I could remember is Dre (my frat brother and security) saying *"dog I got him."* Dre is dragging this dude backwards and I am feeling like I'm in a dream because the harder I tried, I could not get to him. Behind me was Jimbo a 6'1' and close to 350 pound bouncer, holding me. There was no getting away from Jimbo. Jimbo and Dre saved me from going to jail. The inside of my palms and knuckles were bloody from the pavement. I wanted him bad! One thing I have learned is that when security gets tested or thinks he is acting on survival instinct then he becomes like the patrons that need to be escorted out of the club. Now, I am probably one of the more aggressive dudes on the team. I'm not pounding myself on the chest or bragging about something that is not true. I have made it my business to be seen as legit!

I have been trying to strike a balance but I know that what comes in the club is looking for any sign of weakness and I am not trying to show them any signs of weakness. I have learned to be respectful and to practice controlled aggression. I'm sure my day is coming. Any night can be the night that I am cut, stabbed, beaten, or shot. After all, I am dealing with a nation of Cains.

Before going to work, I kiss my wife and daughter. I look at my daughter and say, "always remember daddy loves you." Then I try to erase them from memory because I don't want to think about anything soft or sentimental. I will tune back into that when I get back in my car to go home. My prayer use to be *"my God, please let me handle what I can tonight and whatever I can't, I pray that you cover me."* With that I am secure that I will make it home, but you never know. Over time, my prayer changed to *"God help them."*

These descendants of Cain really hate each other. One thing is for certain, by the time the night is over, black unity turns into a ghost as black males and females become niggas and bitches. Oh you don't like hearing niggas and bitches? Maybe it sounds better if I said a nation of Cains. Cain killed Abel. Once black people hit that switch, become that nigga or bitch or a nation of Cains, there is nothing but hate and a thirst for blood.

Have you ever been in the eye of a storm? The eye is the center of the fight and the storm is the rush of niggas trying to "fuck" somebody up. Well in the middle of that storm are these niggas with faces that have been shaped to represent "evil." You trying to hold off this surge of bad blood with bad intentions but they keep coming and as they hit, kick, stomp, throw bottles, bar stools, pool sticks, and pool balls at the target, there is certainly a lot of love being represented (insert sarcasm of course). Just ask the recipients of those harmful blows, the ones that have eyes, ears, faces, mouths, and teeth that need surgical repair. Ask the countless brothers who lost consciousness or those who can't recognize themselves in the morning.

Indeed, we have a lot of love or a hell of a way of showing it. The biggest brawls have taken place between college fraternity men and local men. In situations where you put them together (i.e. college party), college men are out to steal and maintain the spotlight. The spotlight being the attention of the ladies. The locals are digging the college ladies and want their attention too so they don't respect the men that currently have their attention. Fights often break out as fraternities do their traditional party hops (line steps through the club) and the locals don't move out the way. The locals live for the chaos and of course the college men are out to prove that they are from hoods too. I'm sure the locals have got to understand that if they don't come deep enough to a college fraternity party, then it's a guaranteed ass whooping. Still they try anyway and get beat up badly. Next thing they do is come back prepared and willing to shoot up the place with whatever gun they have stashed in their cars.

There are a good number of black men who come to party and party peacefully. We appreciate peace, some of us would much rather have a non-confrontational night. Admittedly, others on the team live for the battles. Some security are looking for the chance to get physical. If the niggas show up, then we usually get the action we get paid to deal with. Niggas never have identification, never follow the dress code, want to drink and smoke weed in line, and expect that we are going to overlook them because they have money. These fools will pay more just to get in with the wrong clothing on. One dummy paid 100 dollars per timberland boot, so that is two hundred dollars for the shoes, another 100 for the sweat suit and fifty for the hat.

He spent a total of 350 dollars to get in the club, and is not in for longer than 20 minutes. He gets thrown out for smoking weed in the club. Niggas always bring unresolved drama to the club. They strut on that dirty south, get crunk music that seems to not have respect for people or their personal space.

When a fight breaks out, these same niggas don't want to get thrown out of the club. They promise to be cool if we let them stay but what have they created? If it's too out of hand we have to shut the whole party down, which demonstrates no respect for the few that just paid money to get in only to party for a few minutes. Now you have new dudes who just got in and are mad because they paid 20 to 40 maybe more to get in and the promoter(s) is/are hiding out in back somewhere with the money. They don't care they are paid already.

Dudes these days gang fight. I have not seen one, single combatant fight since I've been doing security. These dudes have "group manhood," which is nothing more than individual cowards. They only inflict harm when numbers are in their favor and at other times these same dudes will cut and run. I've seen it! All hard when there are many, and bitch like when you have to face an ass whooping on your own.

Sometimes the blood that spills maybe your own, or your security comrade. On another security night, I had just walked back in the club right before this situation with the "dread" (hairstyle locks, who seems to embrace menacing behavior) happened. I was outside where a young girl had passed out in the parking lot. She was "passed out drunk." All you could see was the whites of her eyes. The owner and I tried to get her to the car. He grabbed her hands and I her feet. Her friends are crying. The dead weight is no joke. This chick is heavy but she is costing me too much time. I'm like watch out, as she lay flat on the ground. I bent over, put my hands under her arm pits and snatched her up. I threw her up and positioned myself to catch her on my shoulder. I did it! She was heavy and hurt my back though. I took her to the car and dropped her drunk, ass in the seat!

Those power exercises in the gym actually work! I'm feeling good, the girls she was with, start "creaming" they want to holler (give you their numbers) but there is no time and I was not interested. I get back in the club and there stands the situation with a "dread."

I have enemies, the kind that want to see me hurt or dead. I promise not to be easy prey though and revenge will be swift. Some people are out to make sure you don't make it home. My job is to get home to the family. We had been putting people out for openly smoking weed in the club. It seemed like we were doing that all night. One guy a "dread head" was caught smoking weed but wanted to buy his way out of being put out of the club. One of our security guys (who led the charge to put him out) told him he does not swing that way. Before I could intervene, the "dread" said something to security that set him off.

The "dread" gets rushed, I grab them both and we smash against the money table. One of the "dread's" partners is rushing in but he is a punk, I stopped him with a quick look and a statement, you better not hit me! He screams control your man! A knife appears and the "dread" gets to security's face. I try to suppress the "dread" without putting my guy at a disadvantage. Security slips, so I grab them both and swing them out the door. I'm wondering why the "dread" is slippery. Security yells, he's got a knife! We struggle for it. It was surreal! All this damn blood! Who is cut! There is blood on my hands! I finally see the knife. I stomp on the "dread's hands" and kick the knife away but it's not far enough, so we rush for the weapon. By this time outside security rushes in and handcuffs the "dread." His damage is done, blood is everywhere but who is cut? My security guy is cut to the face, two wounds from the back of his ear to his chin, deepening at the chin that will require stitches. I rush to the bathroom to wash my hands. They rinse clean, no marks! Damn! I'm tired and my wrist is hurt.

There are times when a security comrade is injured and the injury was fatal. There are times when security has been blessed enough to respond to resuscitation performed by Emergency Medical Services. Under no circumstances are these situations ever forgotten. As stated before they represent nightmares that still haunt me. Shout out to Aaron, I am glad you made it through. I will never forget the language of a man as he processes death, while losing so much blood. Shawn, you are a life savior, fucking field medic. Damn that was the first time, I cried in front of a group of men. I told them, "*if you don't stand with me on this mission to be violent first and ask questions later, then consider tonight your last night, one of us went down and we don't stand for that.*" Thinking back my rise to a leadership role was determined by the right combination of diplomacy and violence but at that moment, diplomacy was no longer an option.

Guns are no joke, gun play is even worse, especially when you can't determine where it is coming from. What you shooting for? It is just a fist fight! Let me tell you, Sucka Free Sundays is straight hood night. It has become a night for brawling with old faces and new bee's trying to get on. Last night, the sounds of clapping fists penetrate the otherwise crisp nighttime air, it is well after 2 am in the morning. The fight spills outside of the club, I'm thinking someone hit my dog, Dre in the face so I'm coming like his wing man.

Dude did swing but missed and Dre had him locked up until dude was like I ain't got no problem with you. Little, another security guy is outside, cliques start jumping the dude Dre just locked horns with. I must say homie handled his but did take a beating, it was just too many guys that wanted a piece of him. The mace that the parking lot security team is using, is ineffective, these fighters are eating it so somebody decides to shoot in the air.

The gun fire was so close to me, I felt a vibration shoot through my body. My ears are ringing and instinct said "move," and I moved quickly for cover. The intent was to clear the area but the consequence was rapid fire return. Now we all in danger of bullets with no names. What you shooting for, it was just a fist fight, these dudes will get tired! At the end of the night, I count my blessings, drive to suburbia, look the family over, walk the dog, and settle down to sleep. It is 4 am, I got to be up in a couple of hours and back to campus by 8 am. Teaching deviance, living through crime and violence, what a way of life.

My kind of club patron is the black woman. The black woman is neatly dressed showing off just enough to tease. They know how to adorn their bodies in a respectful classy way. Even their dance style is one of class. If they do turn around, it's for show and they might let that partner get a feel for how soft they are only to move away in a manner that is lady like. She is a woman for sure. The antithesis of this type of woman is the jezebel, sapphire, hoochie club queen (Collins 2004). She is about the sex. Her sex is on display. She has flesh hanging from every possible opening. Her hairstyle is outrageous. She may even have colored it to match her outfit. She is the kind that will accept a used cigarette from the mouth of some dude she does not even know. Drinking, cursing, and dancing as if she is trying to have sex through her clothes. Try frisking one of these types and you are sure to notice a strange kind of funk on your hands. She may even be a baby mama, with baby mama drama. She is the kind to show out in the club, get kicked out for fighting her baby's daddy or perhaps the woman he is suspected of seeing.

She has a foul mouth and thinks that she can buck up to a dude, smack him and not have him smack her back. Too often, security has thrown out some dude for beating on his girl, and more than likely that same girl will attempt to fight security for throwing the guy that just smacked her out the club. Forget, those type of situations they have to be made for each other.

This jezebel, sapphire, hoochie club queen is a blade carrier. She will keep a blade somewhere on her body, in her shoes, underwear, mouth, hair, and even under her breasts. When all else fails, she is prone to use beer bottles to scar her victims. Jezebel, sapphire, hoochie club queen types are excited about making other females bleed. Her reputation of showing out in the club precedes her. Sadly, many young college females are beginning to mirror jezebel, sapphire, club queen types. They dress the same, dance the same and drink until they are passed out in the parking lot. I've had to put too many in the car or on the flat bed of a pick-up. Their eyes are in the back of their heads. They are peeling away their grace and spirit of life. Why would an African-American Queen want to be a like a jezebel, sapphire hoochie club queen? Could somebody please tell me the answer to that?

The anatomy of the sex subculture on display at adult entertainment clubs is a raunchy affair. The sickest most vulgar act but not all that uncommon are dudes in the club who can't seem to control their sexual impulse and give into the close grinding by pulling out their penis and masturbating on the girl they are dancing with. Often times she is not aware because she had her butt firmly planted on the guy, her face down and hands on the floor. However, once she does realize what happened she is humiliated and pissed. We have no problem throwing these sick dudes out, hell they already had an orgasm and don't resist. Of course, there are clubs for those seeking nudity and an opportunity for random sex.

Down in the valley there is sex if you want to pay for it. Of course there are conventional fronts of what strippers won't do and what you can't get but for the right price you can get whatever you want. It has been advertised far too often that "black sex" is a hot commodity.

The Madam of the strip club bursts over the microphone, *Welcome to Suga Bears. You don't be cheap, get your money out, don't stand around, we got all this pussy. Hot pussy and it ain't free. Hot pussy, the kind that can do whatever, but you cheap motherfuckers have to pay!* There are two goals working. The goal of the stripper and the goal of the patron. The goal of the stripper is to create enough of a fantasy or illusion that the patron can have her so that he spends the most money on her. I have been a private body guard for several adult entertainment dancers and their mantra is *"as long as this nigga think he can fuck he is going to shell out the money."* The patron is thinking that for the right price, the sex will be offered. Some win and some lose. Some men don't mind paying for it and even more strippers don't mind selling it. You can purchase fellatio for 30–50 dollars. Intercourse with only one orgasm for 100–150 dollars. Just ask for the VIP room. Strippers come in all forms. Big, small, short, tall, the darkest of chocolate to the lightest of tan and in between you have the red bones!

Some have smooth skin, others have battle wounds. There are beauties and there are some not so attractive ones but they have the advantage of being voluptuous. You have strippers who do it for the money, for survival, to finance their education, simply for the fame, or it's the only skill they think is marketable. Some do it for the fame too. Not too many seemed to be ashamed. I learned a lot talking to adult entertainment dancers. They were usually very blunt about offering their services. As one noted with confidence *"If you come see me, I will make you cum because my shit is that good. Do you doubt it? For the right price, I suck, I fuck, I swallow, and I spit. I can't make enough just dancing."*

There is such variety of action happening, competing for attention. You got booty shakers, ass clappers, pole stars, stage performers, floor dancers, queens and aspiring stars. Queens can afford to be more selective concerning who they decide to provide a table dance and/or private hands on dance. Hell if you are a good looking man you can pull something out of there and get the sex for free, in fact have her "tip you out." Some clubs are full nudity while others are breast exposure only. Some of the women who attend these spots may be looking to get on. If the club has rejected them or turned down their application for whatever reasons, these women will hang around and undercut the working strippers. By undercutting, I mean they will hang out in the dark places and perform "quickies" (hands beneath the clothes dance experience). Some hang out near the men's bathroom or are in the bathroom to catch those males that want to let "loose" after watching stage performances.

You can get "hands or a blow" for five dollars in the bathroom. The slumming spots, the hole in the wall spots have some straight up special tricks. Some sex bottles, until orgasms and pass them to people (patrons, other strippers) to drink. Hell the sure fire ones drink it themselves. It is called "tastefully done." One booth over you got classic demonstrations of vaginal wall control. Over here she might be puffing and blowing a cigarette with her vagina. Over here this one is shooting pool balls out of her you know what! Over here you might have a two trick performance where some women are eating "corn flakes out of another girl's vagina."

If Tony the Tiger really knew what "frosted flakes, their great!" really meant, he would stop saying it. Over here you might have two women "tossing salad." Dollar, Dollar, Bill! For the love of money that mean, mean green, is what it is all about.

What am I thinking when I am watching all of this? *Boy, don't get caught up, lose focus. Be security, keep a straight face.* Finally, you have the business minded women, who form sex escort clubs. Organized and run by women who described themselves as bisexual. The rational was that a business woman involved in the sex industry does in fact sample the product to increase their ability to advertise the product to clientele. The most popular escort service in Greensboro that frequented and booked clientele out of the more deviant and violent clubs was an escort service called "Good Pussy." An escort service like "Good Pussy" usually employed a scout to keep police officers, and outside security occupied or looking the other way, while the parking lot pimp game was in effect. When I tell you the security game is dirty, scouts were easily identified because they carried a purse full of baby wipes to use after each encounter. The sex industry, even in a small city like Greensboro has a vice grip on plenty of so called law enforcement agents.

The female lock up consists of male strippers. It's commonly known as a "male revue" Let's start with the awful smell. Imagine the smell of sweat, baby oil and the secretions of excitement coming from the women who come to male revues. The place is full, loud music, lights and smoke and the kind of heat that captures the smell, making it a lingering thick mist.

The hype man screams *we got this USDA prime cut beef in here for the ladies. We ain't ashamed to fuck and suck you either. We the real men and we ain't afraid to do nothing. Can we get any volunteers to lay down right here and I guarantee, you will get fucked right now! Any takers? Ladies if you are tired of the little dick men trying to holler, we are here to offer our services, come on in, walk up, look at it, touch it...It's the real deal and we doing it real big!!!*

"Fluff Girls" circle about collecting the money that is thrown at the male strippers. The other duty of "fluff girls" is to perform sexual favors for the dancers to get them ready. They are the hands, mouth, breast, and vaginas that "prep" the dancers for performances. Are they proud of what they do? Well they don't seem to complain. They think what they do is glamorous. Everybody wants to be in some type of industry.

I am being extremely judgmental here but it seems over 50% of the women at these male revues have negative traits so dropping dollars to get sexually aroused is no big deal. Then there are the female strippers there to support the males. The young college girls, as young as 17 and 18 rolling in to see what's happening. The male strippers are extremely kind to that 50% of women who have the negative traits (they make them feel sexually desired). For some it's false advertisement and for others, it's as one dancer stated *"sex for hire."* The goal is the same for male strippers, to create enough of a fantasy or illusion that the patron can have him so that she spends the most money on him. Of course all strip clubs are not the same, the goal of making money and the objectification of women is the common denominator. The caliber of women determine the male and female clientele. My experiences were focused on clubs that attracted the same crowd that frequented the deviant, criminal and violent nightclubs. Some adult entertainment places attempt to distinguish themselves by advertising on bulletin boards, being located on Main Street, and being named a "cabaret."

Many clubs that are human sweat boxes with shifty promoters are terribly deceiving with respect to the patrons. The Hype men are even worse because they set the stage for fights. First rule of thumb, most advertisements promising this or that are simply printed up to get people in line. For example, one flyer that advertises 500 of the hottest wettest ladies, waiting for the fellas to come party is lie. Promotions that suggest that 500 dollars will go to the lady with the sexiest body and swim suit is another common untruth. Here is how the exploitation works. A female decides to enter the contest but the fix is already set up so that she can't win unless she is willing to get completely naked for money. The money goes to the one who is willing to get naked in front of a crowd of men. Shake until sweat drips from private places. Did she enter to do that?

By the way the competition is a stripper that the promoter hired! This is her profession, get naked and shake for men. The promoter is the ultimate judge, so the fix is in. The stripper is the winner, only she gets half the money and the promoter pockets the rest. Thus, female contestants paid to get in the club and entered a contest that was rigged from the start.

Another untruth is on the flyer, which reads "invited guests." An invited guest does not mean confirmed! When a flyer states "hosted by" then the possibility increases that the host will make an appearance. The DJ comes on the Mic and blurts out "such and such will be here in 15 minutes." The promoter and security know these celebrities have not touched base or been in contact with the club to confirm but the DJ keeps saying they are on the way. Here is how it works. If the promoter is not big enough to pay an appearance fee up front (e.g. draft a contract), then there is a guaranteed no show and party goers are not even in the know. Yet, patrons have paid an entry fee that was priced as if the celebrity was actually going to make an appearance.

Another promotion tactic, which is also false is suggesting that the first 100 ladies who are in line before 11 pm will get free drinks. This is highly unlikely because security has been instructed to hold the line, which means only a few will get in by 11 pm. The ones that do, will be served the cheapest, watered down drink possible. The rest of the ladies in line are sheep for the wolves. Yes, they help advertisement, in line looking good, making the club look like it's really packed. Essentially serving as free objectified advertisement.

The promotion game also has "street teams." These are the younger, usually college kids who distribute flyers to promote parties and their only payback is to get in the club free with maybe one or two guests.

The sexual exploitation of female street team members was notable, except it appeared as if female street team members were voluntarily engaged in being exploited. As stated earlier, it appears that everybody wants to be in an industry that carries some type of notoriety even if it is local.

Even more low down and dirty, is when promoters pay some shooters to come shut down a party, so the party goers will go to another location to have fun. It has been known to happen. *"Do me this solid, go fire some shots, clear the competition's parking lot and line. We will be near to offer an alternative place to party."*

And then there is the Hype Man, who may or may not actually be the DJ. The job of the DJ is to entertain the crowd with music for the duration of at least a five hour event. The job is not to insert yourself as the entertainer generating negative energy that sparks fights. Some hype men are known for doing just that but when it is all said and done, security is there for a reason.

The hype man chants:

Where my dirty niggas at? Where my dirty niggas at?
If you got more than a stack (1,000 dollars) in your pocket then put your hands up.
If you getting dirty money, got a nigga on lock down, on probation,
If you don't give a fuck about the police, smoke weed and is fucked up right now? Put your hands up. If you don't give a fuck about nothing then put your middle fingers up, put your middle fingers up!

Ladies, if you got your own job, can pay your own bills, and don't need any of these sorry ass niggas in your life, make some noise? If you got that phat ass and the best pussy in here make some noise. If you are not pregnant or have HIV put your hands in the air and make some noise.

To my niggas, if you like to get your dick sucked, say hell yeah. To my ladies if you like a man to lick your pussy, then make some noise.. Alright now that we are on the same wave. Whose fucking tonight, whose fucking tonight, if you don't give a fuck like we don't give a fuck then put your hands in the air and say oh yeah!!!!!!!!!!!!!

Somebody said, we got New York in the house! Somebody said, we got New Jersey and Philly in the house. Somebody said D.C. and Virginia, Va is in the building. Where my dirty south niggas at????? Fuck that we got North Carolina in the building.

Somebody said, we got tre four, south side in the house.

We got those Aggies in the house, We got the Bells, in the House, Somebody said the Rams are in the house. Somebody said, we got the Spartans from G. Big ups to my college folk but we got the straight up street, hood niggas in the building.

The job of the hype man is to move the crowd, keep the party goers in the groove. They are a mix between radio personalities, and self-proclaimed rap artists. The hype man will do or say most anything to get people to put their hands in the air and make some noise. Once the Hype Man encourages the hood to start representing their respective sets, in addition to playing a minimum of three crunk and/or gangster rap song, security understands immediately that a fight will happen at any moment.

Pivoting to the white affair, involves a variety of music and sometimes live bands. Some of the music playing is at least 10 years old. Security is a bit more relaxed as the usual black guys that act out in other clubs come to white clubs and act more civil. Most white patrons take cabs so they can drink as much as they want. The bar is in to making money not monitoring who had one too many. These white boys are acting out of bounds. They are violating these white girls! *"Homeboy! stay your ass out of the female's bathroom!"* White women and black guys in the same club. What do we have here? It's all in the look. Those that do mess with black guys have that inviting look. Some are quick to tell you all they date are black guys. Black guys wrongly or rightly assume that these white women are more paid than black women, offer less drama, and are easier to get sex from. There are some white women that white men don't want. Some seem to be "breast men" and any white woman that has a little too much butt or hips is usually viewed as too fat.

These body features on a white woman seems par for the course for some black guys who jubilantly announce to their peers *"baby got a phat ass too."* If a white woman is seen as having a body like a black woman then she is a hot commodity and receives much praise. Some black women get jealous, others don't seem to care and will dance with the crew (male or female) that they came with. How many times have you seen a group of black women dancing with one another? Is this a sign of giving up on the brothers? After chasing these white women all night, some black men have the nerve to get mad at black women for holding conversations with those white men that secretly "eye these black women down." It's sort of ironic. These white men don't seem to care for a voluptuous white woman but salivate at the sight of a voluptuous black woman.

The violence at white clubs seem to be watered down when compared to black clubs. Both clubs are subject to have brawls but only one (the black club) has the highest potential to end with someone shooting a gun. At least this has been my experience. It's also been my experience that white males fight until someone goes down and then it is usually over but this is not the case when black males are fighting. The evidence from my observations reveal that black males are intent on doing more damage that does not stop when the combatant gets knocked down or is unconscious.

Going uptown is always a pleasure. The peacefulness of an after hour's spot with the professional black people in town. There is jazz, live music, throwback soul music, comedians, free wings and alcohol. What more could you want? The icing on the cake are the numbers of professional black women in attendance, and looking real nice. Some are just down right attractive, smelling like all kinds of fragrances, with a grown up attitude. They are not even stuck up, well some of them are not. These women seem to be confident and successful.

Black males are typically outnumbered. They should come up in here and see what's really happening. Don't be scared, lay your rap down and see what happens. Another type is the professional married woman suffering from emotional and physical deprivation. These women are looking to "play." They are looking for something to do or someone to do it with. It's not always a sexual thing. Many want to be "courted" again. Romanced, to feel special, not taken for granted, etc., so they turn to the "affair." Dave Hollister sings about "taking care of home." Jaheim, sings about "forgetting to be a lover," perhaps men should listen! These women in here are fiends for attention and men are around to offer them what they think they are missing. Many black women arrive, complete with a good job and a good man so they beaming from head to toe. Smiling from ear to ear, feeling blessed and free from the routine dating game.

Then there are the BWABR's, Black Women with All but the Ring. She has that controlled look. Balancing happiness, offering a mask of contentment but deep down looking for completion. Is there not one good black man left? Well there are many but they have discovered that their good credit, nice car, respectable job, single and heterosexual status places them among the "hunted" so they enjoy being chased by women. More importantly, they seem content with holding their potential status as a carrot of attraction for these black women. The most desperate of these women want a man at all costs resulting in them not caring if a man is already in a committed relationship.

When the celebrities come through it creates such a stirring of preparation. It's amazing to me. I mean do people really feel that strongly about celebrities? During my tenure as a body guard I have witnessed people pass out, cry, take their clothes off, get mad, and fight over a person that is there to collect the money, titillate the fans, then move to the next location.

I've gone from security to body guarding and I have stood next to some of these celebrities. Ladies and gentlemen, these people are regular, normal people, don't idolize them! I know the women with an agenda did not hear that and just want to get near celebrities. Some have even offered me sex just to get them close enough to a celebrity. I'm not that stupid. I may look the part but I am not that stupid. Do you really want to give yourself away for what? Over some time with him, and once you get near him, there is no telling what you are going to do to make an impression. The security/body guard profession has amazed me regarding the freeing of inhibitions during the hedonistic pursuits.

I was working an NBA celebrity party. I won't drop names, but the biggest and probably more famous NBA stars where there. ESPN announcers, actors and actresses were there as well. One of the reasons that I often get selected to body guard big names is because I'm not a fan. I'm there to do a job, not smile in your face or kiss your ass. To be honest 98% of the celebrities are appreciative. In fact, it was that attitude that landed me beside the most popular player to ever dawn an NBA uniform. I'm convinced that some women come there with an agenda. Let me tell you, a woman who throws herself at a man is really hard to resist. I'm not talking about the kind that are drunk, groupies or out of their mind fans. I'm talking about, those that suggest that they don't usually act completely mesmerized, have a significant other but the crush they have on a particular celebrity trumps their normal reality. When they come in with a game plan, some of the celebrities' best made plans for fidelity don't stand a chance.

Then there are the white female fans. You have not witnessed an impassioned hunt until you have seen these women go after these franchise black professional athletes. Black women typically opt out of the competition, and the black professional athletes quickly become hypnotized by the possibility of a one night only sexual encounter.

Again it's in these white female fans' eyes. Many use these athletes to validate themselves. Many black athletes give in, particularly those who have not got a handle on what it means to be chosen. It could be that that these celebrities are just men and get sexually aroused just like any other man. The only difference is that the opportunity for sex is a constant companion.

I'm observing the white men that are here who use their finances to get them close. Still, I can see that they hate to watch these white women throw themselves at these black athletes. I'm close enough to hear what these white women whisper. The evidence is that they are relentless. They have no dignity unless their dignity is closely tied to their promise to "fuck you like you have never been fucked before." Some will stoop to any level. These kind of white women will kiss, and suck up longer than most black women, who prefer to bow out gracefully. It's been said that a black woman will probably do just as much in a bedroom that any white woman would do but she might not put all that business out there right away. It appears from my security tenure that black women are on that non-verbal communication level. They will present their bodies like appetizers. Suggesting that they are just as good as they look. It is then up to the celebrity to determine what is appealing to him. For some white women, you are going to be forced to see her because she will plot to get near you. Some white women are willing to go beyond the point of a black woman who at some point will say "fuck him, he ain't all that." I'm just telling you what I have frequently observed over the course of my security/body guard tenure.

This chapter provided a representative sample of my journaling covering topics related to gangsterism and club night life including violence, sex, differences in club patrons, promotion tricks, duties of a hype man and the different types of party venues I have observed as security, including celebrities I have body guarded. It was a B-side presentation of subject matter, not particularly aimed at establishing any agenda or pushing any theory or methodology. The idea was simply to expose the reader to a shady side of ethnographic research that examines criminogenic gangs, and club night life comprised of deviance, crime, violence and sex.

As stated earlier, the more sociological contributions appear in a book, a research article and two book chapters, I have already published. The major take away here is that participant observation over an extended time period can become more participatory and less observation. If researchers are not careful, the end result will be nothing more than a collection of sentences that failed to decode the cultural codes that are representative of a specific subculture. Moreover, be prepared to be judged by your colleagues and misunderstood by people in your family and social circles. Also don't be shocked by the ethical lines that become blurred nor the discovery of what is attractive. Expect to be caught off guard by something you could not anticipate observing.

My daughter Nia-Faye at some point began to watch the news that would cover stories about security club bouncers being stabbed or shot. She began to openly express concerns about me working. Many times I was able to ease her concerns but would often notice she would be waiting up for me to return home even on some of her school nights. It was time to slow down and eventually become selective about working and then ultimately close out the research project.

I have survived my battles, faced the violence that was meant for me and have performed my duties as a security club bouncer/body guard. I leave the field with a few regrets about the behaviors I engaged in, most notable is the violence. Additionally, I am forever hurt by the senseless murder of more than a few. I have observed too much violence to ever fully enjoy being out at any club. There are several revelations from the sample of B-side notes: (1) engaging in troublesome environments too long can have an adverse impact on the researcher; (2) engaging in security leads to stereotyping and profiling; (3) violence forges identities even amongst personnel that is supposed to be controlling violence; (4) witnessing violence and death is traumatizing and depressing; (5) colleagues, family members and others who come in contact with you during your research will develop suspicions about you; (6) researchers run the risk of becoming too immersed where they seek respectable status from the audience under observation; (7) ending the research does not necessarily mean, freedom from the environment; (8) circumstances observed and level of participation significantly impacts ability to remain objective and divest from the people encountered along the way; (9) personal characteristics factor significantly into ethnographic research, particularly with respect to race and examining deviant populations and subcultures; (10) clubbing is an unhealthy activity because it runs the risk of exposing people to other's deviant, criminal, violent and sexual impression management; and (11) apparently there is no bottom or limit for the hedonistic pursuits of blacks who are equally matched by a clubbing industry that is positioned to provide a place to engage in levels, of deviance, crime, violence and sexual exploits. In closing, I have seen enough and done enough so I am done!

· 7 ·

HULKING OUT

White Males' Response to Bullying, Humiliation, Rejection, Isolation and Perceived Injustice in an Academic Setting

Introduction

Somewhere lurking is a beast, with a pulse quickened by anger over perceived instances of humiliation and injustice. This beast seeks retribution, and is attentive to the moment when people shall hear his roar, feel his might, and absorb his violence. It's a hulking rage that is triggered by an overwhelming sense of shame, and torment that must be acted upon. People who deserve to live will die, and the wounded will be scarred for life. The aftermath is shaken faith, deep sorrow and the search for answers to understand a lethal rampage that came from an unlikely person.

The narrative is becoming all too familiar. The most unusual offenders used lethal violence against unsuspecting victims in unlikely spaces and places. Unfortunately, terrible but justified fears have forced a hasty gravitation towards proclaiming mental illness, which is now the scapegoat for atypical murder. From 1979 to 2014, three hundred and twelve students and faculty members were killed and at least another four hundred and seventy two were wounded.

Elementary, high schools, and college campuses have unfortunately become stages for rampage shootings. The horror of Columbine High school produced fifteen deaths in 1999, which was eclipsed by the tragedy of thirty two deaths on Virginia Tech's campus in 2007, and then there was the un-speakable nefarious event where twenty children were killed in cold blood at Sandy Hook elementary in 2012. Parents, loved ones, and friends were left with a depth of sorrow that even gospel seemingly is reduced to cliché state-ments. In our pursuit of explanations, too many legal agents, social science researchers, and mental health professionals have blamed mental illness as the most significant contributor to these mass murders. However, the social fact is that mental illness does not stand alone as the reason for targeted violence or rampage shootings (Cornish and Clarke, 1986; Fantz, Knight, and Wang, 2014; Fessenden, 2000; Hempel, Meloy, and Richards, 1999; Klein, 2012).

Given males pursue acceptance and respectable status amongst peers, murder becomes an attractive alternative when functional interaction and communication to gain acceptance and recognition has failed. Murderous outcomes could be related to extreme emotional deficits associated with be-ing confronted with circumstances that humiliate, and challenge masculini-ty, devalue human dignity, negate social status, assassinate character, and/or create uncomfortable stress (Fox, Levin, and Quinet, 2005; Gilligan, 1997; Katz, 1988). In other words, when males find themselves marginalized by so-cial institutions, peer groups and/or intimate personal groups with no seem-ingly acceptable way to become meaningful participants, a few males anoint themselves as superior beings, and then gravitate to murder as a cold blooded method of imposing crystal clear messages of "I matter and you don't."

The crux of the matter is that shooting sprees on school grounds are dis-concerting because white males are more likely (than their black male peers) to employ their version of vigilante justice to counter various forms of peer level social dismissal (Kimmel, 2008; Kimmel and Mahler, 2003; McGee and DeBer-nardo, 1999; Rocque, 2012; Schwyzer, 2012).Vigilante justice has gained rela-tive applause in instances where there is a collective understanding that there is a deserving population but has alternatively created moral panic in instances where such behavior has been labeled as killing in cold blood (Estes, 2005; Gilligan, 1997). The actions of rampage shooters, fundamentally implies un-derlying psychological conflicts that manifest as rage; therefore, it's an easy next step to offer mental illness as significantly related to mass murder. However, what if it turns out that rampage shooters rationally deliberate murder, evaluate strategies to sacrifice symbols of their humiliation, and are ultimately satisfied with the finality of life that results from lethal predation? This chapter discusses rampage shootings on school grounds as a product of reasoning criminals who have defaulted to a transformative kill self-mode of operation.

Core Principles of Social Acceptance, Compensatory Reaction and Murder

Family dynamics and family processes are critically important in socializing individuals. The nuances of culture, normative expectations, social development, perceptions, self-esteem and self-efficacy, impact the interpersonal value systems we use to relate to others. As individuals mature, they emerge from the bosom of the family with social, economic, cultural, spiritual, and physical appearance characteristics that will be confronted by diverse institutions, and social networks that present discretionary social value assessments and treatment outcomes relative to confirmation, acceptance, validation, marginalization, isolation and victimization (i.e., deviant, criminal and violent).

When males experience adverse social value assessments and humiliation, they may perceive these experiences as unfair, and be compelled to act on what has now become a social imbalance impeding their happiness and/or comfort levels. Depending on the relentless nature of value assessments and treatment, boys can respond by investing in conventional socially approved methods to achieve relative integration and assimilation, be satisfied with the nuances of their status in the institutional and social network hierarchies, or they can wage a troublesome masculine campaign (actions focused on toughness, self-reliance and taking control of situations using aggressive tactics) to force validation, acceptance and even rejection out of fear (Chatterton 2010; Cohen, 1955; Harro, 2000; McCall, 1994; Oliver, 1989; Rothenberg, 2002; Wallace, 2007).

As soon as boys are presented with opportunities to independently socialize with peers and as soon as boys become enrolled in school, they have to consistently compete for acceptance from peer groups, and academically perform at a sustainable level worthy of grade promotion. For the most part, boys campaign for respect amongst peer groups, and feel a sense of entitled acceptance and academic praise from educational authority figures and teachers by virtue of just being present at school. Make no mistake about it boys mature well into adulthood with a competitive energy and a sense of deservedness. In some cases where campaigns for respect are suppressed and school acceptance is tempered by warranted criticisms and discipline, males (regardless of age) may be inclined to respond with troublesome behaviors. Agnew's General Strain Theory, Gilligan's Saving Face Perspective and the Diathesis Stress Model provide generic assumptions that seem logical enough to explain the use of violence to counter being disrespected by peers, and/or challenged by school authority figures and teachers (Agnew, 2006; Hooley and Gotlib, 2000; Gilligan, 1997).

According to Agnew (2006), the teenage lifestyle carries with it apprehension, angst, uncertainty, frustration, insecurity, and even concern with respect to navigating through social circumstances related to family dynamics, family processes, parent-child relationships, peer group associations, opposite sex relationships, and academic progress. Males (i.e., young boys, adolescent, teenage, young adult, and adult) enthusiastically pursue satisfactory relationships, and acceptable academic performance; however, to the degree that these males experience negative relationships with parents and/or encounter awkward moments with peers, attractive girls, school authority figures, and teachers because of personal attributes and characteristics, they become stressed. The behavioral manifestation will depend on psychodynamic conflicts, personality, definitions of the situation (as humiliating), and problem solving. The generic assumption here is that family, peer group, heterosexual relationships, and academic circumstances can become traumatic events for males who become angry, frustrated, depressed, and ultimately motivated to engage in deviant, criminal and violent behaviors, particularly when there is no evidence of positive counteracting forces to prevent such behavioral outcomes (Agnew, 2006). If behaviors go un-checked, fail to alleviate grief; and/ or does not provide some level of functional balance, then actions can elevate to a mass killing in a public arena that is easily accessible, and provides the largest number of defenseless, unsuspecting, symbolic targets.

Gilligan (1997) contends that routine interactions amongst similarly circumstanced individuals and competing peer groups, contribute to the construction of meaningful social networks, sub-culturally specific normative expectations, and social hierarchies where public persona is a form of social currency that can increase and decrease in value.

Instances where males have experienced functional inclusion, it's likely that they will be conformists or act in accordance to group expectations. Alternatively, when males have encountered circumstances that cause his peers to socially ridicule, scorn, criticize, become socially distant, and devalue his social capital to the point where he is rebuffed and/or has become an outcast, then there is a distinct possibility that he will entertain the idea of becoming violent to offset any perceived loss of peer group approval.

Let me begin with the common empirical observation that people feel incomparably more alarmed by a threat to the psyche or the soul or the self than they are by a threat to the body. The death of the self is of far greater concern than the death of the body...People will sacrifice their bodies if they perceive it as the only way to avoid losing their souls, losing their minds, or losing face… In addition, a person only develops a stable, integrated, and differentiated sense of selfhood or identity through the process of interacting with other humans in the community, or culture (Gilligan 1997, p. 96)*…. I have yet to see a serious act of violence that was not provoked by the experience of feeling shamed and humiliated, disrespected and ridiculed and that did not represent the attempt to prevent or undo this loss of face, no matter how severe the punishment… The purpose of violence is to diminish the intensity of shame and replace it as far as possible with its opposite, pride, thus preventing the individual from being overwhelmed by the feeling of shame. Violence toward others, such as homicide, is an attempt to replace shame with pride* (Gilligan, 1997, pp. 110–111).

These quotes seem to suggest that fatal violence is a defense mechanism against feeling ashamed and/or paranoia about perceptions that peers no longer respect the social legitimacy of a person. Murder seems to be an extreme and unnecessary action; however it is the strongest protest against any agent attempting to bring public shame to the offender. The generic assumption here is that the human spirit thrives under conditions that promote positive social capital (a positive self-image). Hence, when males perceive that their peers have lost respect for them by consistently engaging in behaviors that render shame, and/or whenever males perceive that school officials, and teachers are creating undue hardships then some may turn to murder to regain a sense of superiority (Gilligan, 1997). The targeted areas for murder are most likely public places, and spaces where the murderous desire will garner the most attention.

It logically follows that shooting rampages are ritualistic sacrifices of people that are reduced to offensive objects that have encroached upon the dignified humanity of an offender.

Hooley and Gotlib (2000) offer a succinct examination of the Diathesis Stress Model. The Diathesis Stress Model fundamentally suggests that behavioral outcomes reflect vulnerabilities to specific disorders, and sensitivities to life course events and situational circumstances. In other words, people can be predisposed to mental disorders by virtue of biological factors that are present or developed soon after birth. Mental health can be negatively impacted by stressful events and/or social circumstances that become traumatic enough to effect diminished capacity because people are differently susceptible to environmental conditions, and act based on whether their experiences negatively affect functional thinking, ability to suppress subconscious conflicts and self-regulation. The generic assumption relative to rampage shooters is that males have certain impulses (i.e., selfish pursuits with no regard for reality) that are normally held in check by internal constraints; however, when confronted by traumatic events (e.g., home life, peer group or school experiences that weaken psychological equilibrium), behaviors may no longer yield to morality because subconscious conflicts erupt. Murdering those perceived to be the source of stress seems like a functional alternative because at least the intensity of the trauma is reduced (Hooley and Gotlib, 2000).

Agnew's General Strain Theory, Gilligan's Saving Face Perspective and the Diathesis Stress Model have in common the assumptions that males are confronted, challenged, and exist in social settings that validate, accept, allow for positive identification or can negate respect, suppress identities, challenge entitlements, and cause people to feel insignificant, tormented, and ashamed.

If males experience approval they move throughout life in a mostly conventional way; however if they experience distressing, and traumatic circumstances in the absence of counteracting forces then their behavior may drift towards depravity. Even though, the focus of this chapter has been on males, it should be noted that these very same principles can apply to females who when faced with similar conditions engage in victimless crimes or targeted deviant, criminal, and violent acts, including fatal violence (Agnew, 2006; Hooley and Gotlib, 2000; Gilligan, 1997).

Nature and Extent of Targeted Violence, Mass Murder and Rampage Shootings

Lethal events that encroach upon the serenity of educational institutions underscore the reality that academic settings are not immune to violence. Ultimately, gun violence resulting in death and casualties depends on individuals' motivations, rationalizations, coping strategies, access to firearms, and calculated opportunities (factoring in the degree to which people, and places are prepared to defend against an attack). The circumstances surrounding school shootings appear to be related to the culture of honor, which emphasizes positive social capital related to masculinity (i.e., perceived rights and entitlements to personhood, dignity, respect, praise, acceptance, and social status), pressure moments related to the pursuit of a meaningful existence with family, friends and peer groups in social settings and mental health challenges

(i.e., conditions that interfere with one's ability to effectively rationalize and engage in socially acceptable behaviors) (Agnew, 2006; Hooley and Gotlib, 2000; Gilligan, 1997; Meloy, et al., 2001).

The data from 1979 to 2014 reveal 201 targeted (e.g., specific person defined as the target), rampage (e.g., lethal violence resulting in at least 1 killing and several casualties), and mass murder (e.g., student used firearm resulting in 3 or more murders with several casualties) shooting events with student assailants where 312 were killed and over 472 were wounded (Fantz, et al., 2014; Klein, 2012; McGee and DeBernardo, 1999; Muschert, 2007; Rocque, 2012;). There were an additional 16 campus shootings resulting in several more murders and casualties perpetrated by individuals who were not students. The context for these shooting events was problematic relationships (domestic abuse and jealousy), relationship termination, stalking, and post relationship violence. In these instances shooters were faced with circumstances that proved demeaning to their sense of entitlement to a partner they were currently involved with or the relationship had ended.

Out of the 217 school shootings, 28 happened on college campuses, involving 21 undergraduate and 6 graduate students, and 1 college professor (between 1979 and 2014). In every case, it appears that students and a professor were disgruntled about negative evaluations concerning their academic performance and progress. Undergrad students facing the pressure from parents to perform well in school combined with less than ideal grades, relationship problems, pressures related to sexual orientation, and roommate issues more than likely experienced enough frustration, and stress over their inability to be successful, which led to overwhelming strain. Graduate students responded with lethal violence in retaliation for perceived injustices related to professors negatively evaluating their classroom performance, writing and research ability. Additionally, graduate students generally believed that they were far more capable than their grades reflected, and responded with violence in those instances where they were dismissed from the program.

In the single case involving a female professor at the University of Alabama, 3 professors were murdered, and 3 others were wounded during a faculty meeting. It was determined that her motive was denial of promotion and tenure. Obviously the professor felt academically disrespected, entitled to tenure, and perceived that those who did not support her promotion to tenure created an unjust hardship (Fantz, et al., 2014; Klein, 2012).

When compared to homicides involving firearms in neighborhoods, public places and work settings, school yard and campus shootings are a rare occurrence. Nevertheless, the dramatic nature, media coverage, and public concern manufactures a moral panic. Targeted school violence weakens collective faith in social regulation and control (Katz, 1988; Langman, 2009; Muschert, 2007). There were 8 targeted school shootings with at least 1 dead, several wounded and a suicide (7 of which were self-inflicted and 1 was suicide by cop). Additionally, there were 9 instances where a student went on a shooting rampage resulting in mass murder (3 or more killed), with casualties and a suicide (all self-inflicted) (Klein, 2012). In these cases students experienced problematic socializing happenstances where they were deemed outcasts and thus became desperately isolated, and perhaps convinced that their reputation was beyond repair in a manner that would be acceptable to those peer groups they felt were critical to their happiness (Andriolo, 1998; Kalish and Kimmel, 2010; Larkin, 2008; Preti, 2006).

High school shootings (100 cases) were more common than elementary (17 cases), middle school (24 cases) and college campus (16 cases) between 1979 and 2011 (Klein, 2012). Males more than females, overwhelmingly (95%) participated in school shootings.

The data indicate that perceived challenges to masculinity and relationship troubles (i.e., arguments, abuse, break-ups, and jealousy) were identified as possible antecedents to school shootings 70% of the time and grievances with school authority figures were identified as possible causes to school shootings 30% of the time. Challenges to masculinity came in the form of verbal and physical bullying, fighting, stealing, destroying personal property, attempts at character assassination by gossiping and taunting about clique affiliations, sexual orientation, and the over-all perception that an enemy has been created because of some level of perceived cruelty. Relationship troubles included arguments, abuse, break-ups, jealousy, stalking, and the overall perception that girls are not supposed to reject boys. Grievances with teachers included disagreement over graded assignments, and the perception that a teacher had embarrassed a student in front of his peers. Additionally, school shooters seemed to have adverse reactions to instances where they felt judgments at their school hearings were biased, and had problems with accepting or adjusting to disciplinary actions related to in-school suspension or suspension from school grounds altogether (Kimmel, 2008; Kimmel and Mahler, 2003; Larkin, 2007; Leary, Kowalski, Smith, and Phillips, 2003; Newman, et al., 2004; Vossekuil, et al., 2002).

Agnew's General Strain Theory and Gilligan's Saving Face Perspective similarly suggest that social network dynamics, processes and circumstances operate to impact individuals in ways that affect behavioral outcomes. Agnew's General Strain Theory implies that individuals may be inclined to sever ties from conventionalism and engage in drastic behaviors when they experience events that threaten their dignity (Agnew, 2006). Gilligan's Saving Face Perspective implies that seeking masculine identities involve investing in a culture of honor that emphasizes being in control of structural, and situational circumstances in a manner befitting of respect (Gilligan, 1997).

A logical assumption derived from General Strain Theory and the Saving Face Perspective would be that males are likely to act out when confronted by events that cause his peers to devalue his social capital to the point where he is disrespected, rejected, or made fun of in public. The data shows that school shooters were males who experienced direct assaults to their manhood (i.e., masculinity, relationship troubles, and problems with school authority figures); hence, it's logical to conclude that rampage shootings have been used as a mechanism to reclaim some measure of respect, overcome embarrassment, and to get back at specific persons or people who represent a symbol of his humiliation (Agnew, 2005, 2006; Gilligan, 1997; Felson, et al., Allen, South, and McNulty, 1994).

Race and Killing Moods

Living in a violent society with access to lethal weapons provides ideas and resources to carry out fatal revenge on designated targets. This country has been witnessing males turn to violence as a means to problem solve in cases where they have not been accepted, are experiencing challenges to their dignity, and/or are finding themselves having to exist outside of important peer groups. In other words, as males seek to negotiate their manhood within their respective social arenas, they are relatively prepared to handle social challenges, competition, and obstacles preventing a comfortable transition to achieving respectable social status. The seemingly incomprehensible acts of targeted violence, and rampage shootings resulting in casualties and mass murder (on primary and secondary school grounds, and on college campuses across the country) has generated public concern, and unsettling fear as these terrorists-like events are being largely committed by suburban white males.

The most notable of rampage killings resulting in mass murder and suicide were Columbine in 1999 (two White male shooters), Virginia Tech in 2007 (an Asian male shooter), Sandy Hook in 2012 (White male shooter), and Isla Vista in 2014 (assailant self-identified as Euro-Asian). In 2008, a young African-American woman (not a student) went on a rampage killing 3 in Baton Rouge Louisiana. A roll call of rampage shootings on school grounds from 1996 through 2008 suggest that white males (17) were triggermen in school shootings in Moses Lake Washington, Bethel Alaska, Pearl Mississippi, West Paducah Kentucky, Stamps Arkansas, Jonesboro Arkansas, Edinboro Pennsylvania, Springfield Oregon, Littleton Colorado, Conyers Georgia, Fort Gibson Oklahoma, Santee California, New York New York, Red Lion Pennsylvania, Cold Spring Minnesota, Jacksboro Tennessee, and Cleveland Ohio. A school shooting in Dover Delaware was committed by a black male (Rocque, 2012). Other studies examining rampage shootings have concluded that there is a tendency for white males more than black males or white and black females to engage in school shootings (Kimmel, 2008; Kimmel and Mahler, 2003; McGee and DeBernardo, 1999). It's safe to suggest that rampage shootings are more likely to occur in low crime suburban and rural areas, which may speak to why shootings are more likely to be carried out by white males. However, when dealing with targeted acts of violence on school grounds, such school shootings where there is a specific grievance between minority combatants are more likely to be carried out on inner city school yards (Casella, 2001; McGee and DeBernardo, 1999; Newman et al., 2004; Rocque, 2011).

In spite of having a good deal of data for why school shootings occur, there is a hesitancy to offer a one size fits all profile for rampage shooters. Social science theories can only offer educated guesses regarding the potential for a person to engage in a school shooting.

Biological, psychological, and sociological theories have cast a wide net by offering pre-dispositional risk factors (e.g., mental health issues, psychodynamic conflicts and personality traits) and social context variables (e.g., private home troubles, peer group interaction, conflict issues, and contempt and condemnation for school officials) (Fast, 2008; Langam, 2009; Larkin, 2007; Leary et al., 2003; Newman et al., 2004; Vossekuil et al., 2002). Similarly biological, psychological, and sociological explanations have been used to indirectly explain racial differences in school shootings (Rocque, 2012). Upon closer inspection, answers to racial variation in shooting perpetrators, perhaps can be gleaned from differential socialization between white and black males. Generally speaking, in a white patriarchal society, white males may benefit from white privilege (an ascribed social credit that reinforces positive self-esteem, acceptance, and access to life chances that promote life course success). White privilege promotes intra-racial confidence because socially approved institutions, and social structures appear to be geared towards advancement. More specifically, white privilege is favored racial inclusion, and assumes that white males have an inherent ability to carve out an acceptable, and reasonably respectable identity as well as achieve social, academic, financial, and employment success. Essentially, white privilege is a cultural context that bolsters notions of entitlement because of racial supremacy, integrity, intellectualism and deservedness (Rothenberg, 2002). Institutional challenges to assumed intellectualism, and/or peer group rebuffing creates a disjunction between the benefits of white privilege and reality of circumstance. Hence, when white privilege is negated this could lead to troublesome behavioral outcomes particularly in instances where white males are rejected, criticized, marginalized, and/or made to feel insecure, uncertain, ashamed and indignant.

White males attempting to remedy their marginalized status turn their personal problems of adjustment to a community problem in those instances where they chose to target symbols (schools, school officials, and peer groups) of their social down fall. Parents can become targets too, particularly when white males feel their parents have been inept in preparing them for the re-alities of life. In other words, it logically follows that when white males expe-rience negative experiences that counter the advantages of white privilege, they may perceive these experiences as an unjust campaign that undermines their humanity. Essentially, stressed, strained, traumatized, and feeling awk-ward with no directives on how to remedy their situation, may lead some white males to identify with rampage shooters because they view them as warriors, avengers or heroes (Fox et al., 2005; Langam, 2009; McGee and DeBernardo, 1999; Sullivan and Guerette, ,2003).

African-Americans' legacy in this country includes, systematic denial of citizenship rights, inequitable justice as well as psychological warfare on the humanity of blackness (Cleaver, 1996; Cureton, 2011; Dyson, 1996; Haley, 1964; Levin, 2002; Magida, 1996). Moreover, in a white patriarchal dominant society black males have encountered black caste codes (an ascribed con-dition focused on blacks' criminality), which fosters suspicion, moral panic, threat, fear, and the type of opportunity channeling that negatively impacts self-esteem, and restricts life chances leading to less than ideal social, academ-ic, employment, cultural, economic and legal sanction outcomes (Alexander, 2010; West, 2001; Wilson, 1987, 2009).

Given there are varying degrees of racial acceptance, tolerance, challenge, rebuffing, suppression, oppression, discrimination and alienation, expressions of black masculinity will differ from expressions of white masculinity (Ander-son, 1999; Cureton, 2011; Cureton and Wilson, 2012; Estes, 2005; Williams, 2004; Wilson, 1987, 1996). African-American families (middle, working and lower class) have to socialize their children in a manner that equips them with the necessary tools to successfully navigate the demands of convention-al society and mainstream institutions as well as the normative expectations attached to intra-racial subcultures operating in their neighborhoods and social networks (Anderson, 1990, 1999; Chatterton, 2010; McCall, 1994). Dysfunctional family dynamics and family process circumstances create family pressure, and failure to address the stresses related to negotiating black personhood. Whenever the family falls short on providing acceptable ways to adjust to institutional and social network challenges, black males will seek out alternative ways to defend themselves. Specifically, black males contend with estimations of their criminality from educational institutions, which take the form of negative labeling, unwarranted attention, value assessments, and strict disciplinary actions in the classroom, in school suspensions or out of school suspensions. In an effort to counter their displeasure with these circumstances, black males respond by adopting a nonchalant attitude, uncaring disposition, and perhaps a gravitation away from the perceived benefits of academic success. Consequently, black males rebel against schools and invest in subcultures that provide avenues for success that devalue the merits of education (Cohen, 1955; Katz, 1988; Majors, 1993; Nirvi and Maxwell, 2012; Wilson, 2009).

Another immediate concern for black males is having to confront immediate challenges to their respectability (earned social status within peer groups), and having to vigorously proclaim and defend masculine status. Associating, affiliating, and identifying with deviant, criminal and/or violent subcultures that emphasize aggressive manhood provides normative expectations that are consistent with street codes, street elitism and gangsterism. Blacks males are expected to adopt a set of rules that promote violence as a way to problem solve or settle grievances with perceived combatants (Anderson, 1990, 1999; Cureton, 2002, 2008, 2010, 2011; Cureton and Wilson, 2012; Katz, 1988; Oliver, 1989; Wallace, 2007). To the degree that black males invest in subcultures that focus on earning social status away from the confines of school, and negotiating a cool pose to combat school rejection, they are less likely to engage in rampage shootings on school grounds compared to white males who identify with classroom avengers. Additionally, black males who subscribe to street codes or gangsterism may engage in targeted violence against clearly defined persons more so than revenge violence against anonymous people, who represent a symbol of personal dissatisfaction. (Canetto, 1997; Majors, 1993; McGee and DeBernardo, 1999).

The take away from this racial examination of responses to school experiences and peer interaction is that both white and black males condemn school officials for actions taken against them, and both white and black males respond to peer group challenges. However, the differences in racial responses appear to be related to contextual socialization, white privilege for white males, and black caste codes for black males. White privilege indirectly creates a chasm of undefined ways to counter rejection, and black caste codes indirectly creates a defined set of subcultural meanings to counter rejection.

It could be argued that differences in socialization lead to differences in lethal violence on school grounds. It would prove beneficial for school officials to become culturally aware of differences in socialization because the psychological definitions that take root in white and black boys' lives could very well represent the difference between rampage shootings, and targeted violence. It is not safe to assume that by the time white males reach college they have successfully dealt with the pitfalls of white privilege, and that black males have overcome the adverse effects of black caste codes. It's also not the case that institutions of higher learning are exempt from labeling, judging, rejecting, challenging, marginalizing, and disciplining in objectionable ways. Therefore, institutions of higher learning have to answer the call to create a thoroughly comprehensive inter-racial environment with tangible evidence of diversity as well as gender sensitive (male and female) instruction, guidance, and counseling. Colleges and universities can either embrace an improved effort to address the nuanced needs of its male population or brace for the impact of mass lethal violence on their campuses.

Note on Mental Illness

The cold blooded senseless nature of lethal violence aimed arbitrarily at symbols resulting in rampage shootings, mass murder, and suicide shocks the collective conscience, creates moral panic, and fear that there is little control over motivated offenders who intend to inflict wholesale devastation. Atypical killings in public places often force public figures to pursue immediate answers, without the full set of social facts concerning the event. A significant amount of energy is dedicated towards aligning rampage shootings resulting in mass murder, and suicide with mental illness.

An examination of research reveals that 50% to 67% of targeted lethal violence, and rampage shootings resulting in mass murder and suicide have been attributed to a mental health component inclusive of probable psychosis, adjustment disorders, mood disorders, delusional disorders, depression, schizophrenia, mental health trauma (resulting from disruptive events) and diagnosed diminished capacity conditions requiring professional counseling, prescription medication and/or mental health facility treatment. However, when identifying a history of diagnosed mental health pathologies and/or disease that requires professional attention as a precursor to rampage shootings, the number of instances decrease from as high as 67% to somewhere between 11% and 15% (Dikel, 2012; Hooley and Gotlib, 2000; Rocque, 2012).

In most cases, there is much speculation about a rampage event, after the fact whereby a host of professional and legal agents, along with politicians, and peer group associates chime in offering ad hoc explanations as to why the perpetrator used lethal violence as a means to an end. It's far too easy to review rampage shootings as the result of psychosis, diminished capacity, loss of contact with reality, impaired insight, and/or hallucinations of a better existence because these thoughts in and of themselves are not necessarily deviant but become elevated as illogical musings when they are acted upon in non-conventional ways. The moral panic becomes somewhat calmed when the public can be convinced that mental illness is the stand alone culprit in rampage shootings (Fessenden, 2000; Hempel et al., 1999; Langman, 2009). Explaining rampage shootings as the result of individuals breaking from reality, severing emotional connections, and suffering from an emotional breakdown, certainly restores some degree of comfort as the public may be inclined to think that controlling, regulating, and treating mental disorders prevents cold blooded senseless murder.

The social scientific method of evaluation should include an examination of the relationship between prior mental health issues and rampage shootings. Additionally, there is much to be gained from examining the impact of adverse social factors, events, and circumstances on lethal predation in public places and spaces. In order to effectively address the problems that males are experiencing, it is necessary to examine the probability that rampage shooters rationally explored the realities of their actions, and became comfortably resigned to the fact that imposing the death penalty on people, and causing others to suffer is justly warranted (Gilligan, 1997; Katz, 1988). How scary would it be if it turns out that rampage shooters are less likely to be suffering from mental health issues, and are more likely to be reasoning criminals? It's a probable fact that rampage shooter sacrifice life in order to gain re-entry into peer conversations that had been exclusionary, or to cure an imbalance brought on by perceived injustices, unfair criticisms, rejection and denial. Rampage shooters in similar fashion to conventional citizens may not be suffering from anything other than wanting to matter; however, the major difference is using murder (after some degree of processing social facts, strategic analysis, and opportunity assessment) as some form of social currency. If the goal is to increase academic setting safety, then there are implications that should be acted upon when rampage shooters are understood as suffering from mental health issues or determined to be deliberate thinkers who rationally process information, and decide to intentionally kill in mass (Cornish and Clarke, 1986; Gilligan, 1997; Katz, 1988; Tuck and Riley, 1986).

Jack Katz's Theory of Righteous Slaughter

Jack Katz's theory of Righteous Slaughter, offers a reasonable analysis of a typical homicide because the theory embodies core questions (e.g., what are the killer's motivations, relative to the victim, how will his actions solve the problem, and what significant social facts make the scene an appropriate place to carry out the crime?) that speak to rampage shootings carried out on school property. Just as Gilligan (1997) posits that violence results from an individual attempting to regain respectful consideration in the eyes of his intimate social circle after suffering some measure of disgrace; Katz (1988) argues that individuals will use murder to sacrifice individuals perceived to have infringed upon their rights to exist free from ridicule, slander, and/or challenge to personhood. Essentially, Gilligan (1997) and Katz (1988) seem in agreement that murder is a reasonable outcome to seize respect from people perceived as deeply offensive in a humiliating manner.

Jack Katz (1988) argues that a righteous slaughter (murder) serves the purpose of protecting socially acceptable statuses. Katz contends that social groups believe that every person is entitled to socially approved goods (e.g., manhood, womanhood, respect, love, and family). In the event that any one of these are threatened, ridiculed, or harmed by another person, the response would be an emotional reaction that runs the risk of being lethal, especially if humiliation is involved. According to Katz, when a person is humiliated (feels the burden of a character assassination), he/she may free fall into rage (an overwhelming emotional imbalance where one is propelled by blinding anger), which then leads to engaging in chaotic behavior (conduct that falls outside the boundaries of conventionalism) resulting in sacrificial violence (the source of humiliation is eliminated) (Katz, 1988).

Recall that the ingredients for high school, and college campus shootings involve the contextual realities of differential socialization relative to white privilege and black caste codes, problematic socializing happenstances resulting in desperate isolation, and some level of awareness that reputations have suffered excessive damage. Precursors to lethal predation involved perceived challenges to masculinity and relationship troubles (i.e., verbal and physical bullying, arguments, abuse, break-ups, and jealousy), attempts at character assassination through gossiping, and taunting over clique affiliations, sexual orientation, and the over-all perception that an enemy has been created because of some level of perceived torment. Additionally, school shooters seemed to have adverse reactions to grievances with grade assessments, educational progress in challenging programs, instances where they felt judgments at their school hearings were biased, and had problems with accepting or adjusting to disciplinary actions related to school suspensions (in school or suspended from school grounds altogether) or dismissal from undergraduate and graduate level programs (Andriolo, 1998; Kimmel, 2008; Kalish and Kimmel, 2010; Kimmel and Mahler, 2003; Larkin, 2007; Leary et al., 2003; Newman et al., 2004; Preti, 2006; Vossekuil, et al., 2002).

All of the above circumstances can lead to humiliation setting off a chain reaction resulting in rampage shootings, mass murder and suicide. It is very possible that any combination of the above mentioned circumstances can become so devastating and reach a tipping point whereby an individual loses sense of self value and/or becomes overwhelmingly bitter enough to be propelled in to a kill self-mode.

Once humiliation has reached the depths of despair as to ignite the kill self-mode, some males may become intent on killing tormentors as well as themselves in an effort to reclaim some measure of dignity, while simultaneously sacrificing a part of the self that allowed the humiliation to happen in the first place. Essentially, in life and death, he becomes resigned to the fact that the narrative of his life will become far more meaningful after the murder and suicide than it is now or that his social currency will be elevated from victim to superior predator. Even though he will not be around to experience the changing narrative, the thought of it sustains him enough to carry out the act (Canetto, 1997; Gilligan, 1997; Katz, 1988; Preti, 2006; Range and Leach, 1998; Stack and Wasserman, 2009).

Educational Institutions Become the Stage for the Grand Finale

Education is significantly related to improved life chances, and academic settings are in many ways social arenas where individuals have to demonstrate an ability to negotiate socially acceptable status, and strive to achieve academic success. In cases where students experience functional peer group inclusion, and achieve academic success, school is perceived as the best of times. Alternatively, when students are rejected by their peer groups, marginalized, made to feel insignificant, and are unable to successfully overcome academic challenges, then school perhaps becomes the worst of times. Perceived social exclusion, humiliating social experiences, negative evaluations from teachers, unwarranted attention from school officials, the threat, and/or pending dismissal from school grounds or academic programs generates stress, anxiety and strain leading students to defer to vigilante actions aimed at settling social disputes and perceived injustice.

As students proceed into advanced stages of their education, failure to successfully integrate with socially approved groups and/or inability to handle the demands of college courses elevates tension as graduate and undergraduate students may perceive failure as detrimental to their goals to secure the American dream. The majority of students take advantage of the numerous resources to improve their college experience; however, a few drift into despair, and use violence as a method to transcend failure (Gilligan, 1997; Katz, 1988; Langam, 2009; Levin and Fox, 2001; McGee and DeBernardo, 1999; Sullivan and Guerette, 2003).

Institutions of higher learning (similar to high schools) while designed to prepare students for entry into a phase comprised of establishing a lifestyle of significant friendship networks, romantic relationships, job security, resources, and material acquisitions necessary for supporting a family can become a source of contempt. Institutions are microcosms of society utilizing curriculum instruction, governing bodies, culture, honor codes, and diverse social networks to provide opportunities for students to become well rounded citizens. However, these very same components can be perceived as creating academic courses that unfairly rank students' intellectual ability, and social atmospheres that devalue inter-personal skills. Institutions of higher learning perhaps take for granted that their diverse majors, campus life activities, campus groups, counseling services, student out-reach programs, and professor-to-student rapport provides a fundamentally sound college experience while at the same time serving as enough of a safety net for troubled students. The flipside is that the college environment while providing numerous opportunities for inclusion inherently has just as many opportunities for students to be confronted by exclusion leading to alienation.

The narrative for rampage shootings on school grounds reveals issues with personal accountability, jaded perceptions of reality, image construction flaws, and a need to elevate to superior status by lethal means (Fast, 2008; Langam, 2009; Larkin, 2007; Leary et al., 2003; Newman et al., 2004; Vossekuil, et al., 2002). High schools, colleges, and universities have undergone significant changes relative to prevention of and preparedness for rampage shootings, since the mass murder events at Columbine in 1999 and Virginia Tech in 2007. Additionally, given, the increased attention to high school and campus shootings, the Secret Service along with the Department of Education has worked diligently to develop a Safe Schools' Initiative. The blueprint seems to be proactive, and reactive to the reality that no academic setting is immune to rampage shootings. The prevailing theme aimed at prevention seems to be anchored in information gathering and campus security (Vossekuil et al., 2002). Information gathering is extremely critical in prevention because it involves collaborative efforts from mental health professionals, local law enforcement, campus security, school administrators, staff and professors. Mental health professionals, counselors and perhaps professors have to tune into potential shooter's motivations, which is difficult to ascertain without having consistent contact with potential shooters. In spite of the difficulty, the Secret Service has developed a framework for threat assessment or a method by which facts about a potential threat are gathered (by mental health professionals, and counselors) and used to prevent a potential attack (Reddy et al., 2001; Vossekuil et al., 2002). Anytime there are attempts to assess criminality, and predict the actions of would be criminals there is the potential for discretionary actions (i.e., labeling, profiling, channeling opportunities, engaging in unwarranted surveillance and information sharing) (Reddy et al., 2001). However, there has to be some element of trust that threat assessments will proceed with the ultimate goal of risk assessment and prevention.

Moreover, with the understanding that crimes occur with the convergence of motivated offender and opportunity, schools and campuses have been making efforts to increase environmental surveillance, secure otherwise unguarded areas, increase law enforcement presence, have law enforcement and school personnel engage in active shooter exercises, and ensure that emergency alert systems are efficiently disseminated to students, and faculty (particularly for college campuses). Unfortunately, schools and campuses have so many free spaces or unprotected locations, that it will always be difficult to completely eliminate the risk of a shooting event (Rocque, 2012; Reddy et al., 2001; Vossekuil, et al., 2002).

Conclusion: Safety Checks and Balances

What more can educational leadership do to deter individuals from carrying out rampage shootings given it's almost impossible to know with certainty the intentions of motivated offenders? This may seem very basic but a potential solution rests with educational seminars that train ground zero persons (i.e., professors, advisors, residence hall counselors, and other individuals who have consistent contact with students) to become more aware of student motivations. Seminars could certainly emphasize Agnew's General Strain theory, Gilligan's Saving Face Perspective, differential race socialization (e.g., white privilege, black caste codes, cool pose, and code of the street) and Katz's Righteous Slaughter Perspective (Anderson, 1999; Agnew, 2006; Alexander, 2010; Gilligan, 1997; Katz, 1988; Rothenberg, 2002; Wilson, 2009). Additionally, perhaps the presence of full-time social network specialists (who would examine all things social media related to the institution, monitor social networking patterns of students, and research grapevine posted material), college experience coaches, (similar to life coaches whose job it is to monitor the academic and social dynamics of college students), student anonymous reporting call in centers (similar to crime stoppers), troublesome relationship and/or grievance hotlines (similar to call centers concentrating on domestic abuse, alcoholism and suicide), faculty, peer sponsors, peer level mentors (who are perhaps affiliated with diverse socially accepted groups), and campus safe/inclusivity zones could prove significant in preventing school massacres. In terms of community outreach, perhaps a small community/school center where parents or legal guardians of students are welcome to routinely visit campus, accompany their sons/daughters to classes, and even a reversal of rules prohibiting disclosure of students' grades to parents could be a step towards deterring school shootings on college campuses. Also, it could make a difference if there were public places known for professor/student gatherings where professors and students could mingle naturally over breakfast and lunch. Furthermore, high schools and universities should invest more time in exchange programs where professors guest lecture in high school classrooms and/or college bound students are allowed to visit select classes in order to be exposed to the college experience.

More and more colleges and universities are becoming saddled with budget issues, and administrative functions that seem to be turning schools into business operations. It may be time to return to embracing the reality that as educational agents, duties will have to include, teaching students, assisting with a student's well-being, and risk management (this holds true for high school teachers as well). If our schools and colleges are already being proactive in the areas mentioned above then they are on the right path to reducing the potential for a rampage shooting. Unfortunately, even with all the safe guards in place (i.e., the blueprint for threat assessment, target hardening, campus preparedness, and educational leadership awareness) there simply is no such thing as a full proof plan to prevent rampage shootings because human nature is unpredictable.

However, it remains a daily duty to provide a healthy and safe environment for learning, and after all the consistent hard work, the reality remains that every time violence bypasses schools, so many people are blessed to continue their life's journey. Finally, even though prayer is relatively objected to in schools, prayer just might be a necessary ingredient for prevention.

Research Note: Without Sanctuary or Leisure, Moving in on Soft Targets

Emanuel African Methodist Episcopal Church in Charleston, South Carolina has a storied legacy of survival, spirituality, and strength that makes it a pillar in the black community. On June 17, 2015, a 21 year old white male motivated to start a race war, entered the church and engaged in a nefarious deed ending the lives of 9 African-Americans who were in attendance for Bible study. This mass murderer made sure that 9 African-Americans would have no sanctuary for worship and prayer. The nation was encapsulated in disbelief, and mourned in a manner that erased racial lines of division. Politicians and leaders offered familiar narratives of condolences and embraced routine rhetoric focusing more on the forgiving nature of black people. Unfortunately, it was all a routine ending in turning the page in similar fashion to what was done in 2012 when 20 beautiful children were murdered at Sandy Hook Elementary School in Newtown, Connecticut. Currently, movie theatres and/or places of leisure have become soft targets where mass murderers can get maximum results before facing an equitable defense that could effectively thwart their attack. Additionally, social media has become part of the equation where violence has found a way to stream into our everyday lives. On August 26, 2015, a disgruntled gunman, two years removed from his job as a news reporter murdered two former co-workers while they were broadcasting a story live at Smith Mountain Lake in Moneta, Virginia. This gunman then went on to reach out to the public declaring a sadistic victory over some perceived injustice before committing suicide.

Again, America finds itself in a state of shock relative to the cold-blooded nature of a killing from a person who was on nobody's radar when it came to lethal targeting. It seems we are living in a time where it's logical to suggest that home grown terrorism has invaded American's routine activities. Therefore, there is a desperate need to address variables related to socialization, personal motivations, mental health, and the psychological processes operating in the minds of individuals that prove related to mass murder in sanctuaries, movie theatres, and other public places and spaces. It could very well be that the steps needed to protect America's student population are also necessary to protect people in the work force and the general public.

· 8 ·

A LOVE OF OUR OWN

The Manner in Which Black Men Love

There is enough literature and social discourse aimed at the social construction of black women, inclusive of casting negative dispersions and highlighting marriage suitability. For reason that non-flattering narratives of black womanhood saturates the cultural market, this chapter will instead focus on the relationship between black men and black women as an apocalyptic fusion. More, specifically, the focus will be on the gender inequality dogma a disproportionate number of black men from virtually every social class, seems to trumpet. Cleaver contends that Africans who became black in America experienced "primeval mitosis," a splitting of energy and a severing unity of spirit starting with slavery, and carrying through integration and assimilation, which was followed by an "apocalyptic fusion," a desperate and troublesome attempt to reunify as essential companions (Cleaver, 1968, p. 207). The black man and black woman shared a pure African element (nucleus of a union of energies) that was physically separated by slavery and consciously split by colonization (evidence of a primeval mitosis). The apocalyptic fusion, the attempt by black men and black women to establish and maintain a functional relationship is problematic because of polarizing gender roles, and relationship practices that appear to be offensively contradictory (Cleaver, 1968, 218; Cureton and Wilson, 2012, p. 10).

This chapter assumes that black women are inherently beautiful, with tangible and intangible qualities, attributes, traits and characteristics that make them worthy of functional love by choice, not by default. There are millions of black women that are grace personified and at no time have these millions of black women declined from being favorable and worthy of being loved by men who are primarily interested in helping them achieve their fullest potential. Certainly, I am not speaking in absolute terms but I am suggesting that black women's chronicle of love and sacrifice more likely than not reveals that they are paragons. From this point forward, referring to black men and black women should be taken to mean a significant enough proportion of them have functioned in a manner that warrants attention.

There is no denying that millions of black men have a troublesome history of loving black women to their disappointment more than their satisfaction and contentment. Black men have at times been bad actors posing as committed relationship companions, only to end up trespassing over the hearts of black women. Social affirmation movements reveal a history of black men demanding and expecting that black women sacrifice their existential pursuits in favor of helping black men substantiate a patriarchal figure head comparable to white men (Beale, 1970; Dyson, 1996, 2000; Wanzo, 2011). Black men have yielded to temptations, seized upon emotional comfort in spite of their relationship status, and found themselves captivated by women other than their significant others for reason that the other woman is a vessel for renewal, rejuvenations, discovery and a new chance to be validated. Perhaps it is as simple as a fresh pair of eyes gazing upon black men, an escape from relationship pressures and strains or the opportunity to peel back layers of pain without the same fear of having that pain take center stage at home during arguments.

One essential question becomes, which woman is helping this man successfully negotiate, navigate, and maintain his masculinity in a dignified manner? Another question is who does he turn to for emotional and physical communion with the least amount of turbulence? Essential companions (partners that complete one another) are sometimes passed over in lieu of entertaining the company of the woman who offers the path of least resistance.

Alternatively, some black men have been committed to a functional love that aids in positioning black women to fulfill their economic, educational, cultural, familial, and spiritual destiny. Black men have loved loyally and completely, been reliable and disciplined husbands, and fathers, and relatively successful at instrumental and expressive love. Instrumental love is taken to mean assisting with building and maintaining a household and expressive love is taken to mean tangible and intangible behaviors that affirm a woman as his foremost companion whom he professes to have an exclusive set of intense feelings (Webster and Rashotte, 2009). Apparently, for far too many black women, this type of loving black man has traditionally been in short supply.

The tradition of black men loving black women has never been free of obstruction. What's more the legacy of the black experience, inclusive of institutional, cultural macro and micro blueprints designed to cast black women as possessing un-exploitable sexual passion and black men as sexually undisciplined and depraved has led to black men and women turning on one another in socially harmful ways.

> Cleaver states: The white stood between us, over us around us. The white man was your man and my man. Do not pass lightly over this truth, my Queen..It is to be pondered and realized in the heart, for the heel of the white man's boot is our point of departure, our point of Resolve and Return—...I can't bear to look into your eye. Don't you know (surely you must have noticed by now: four hundred years!)...That is the unadorned truth. Not that I would have felt justified under the circumstances, in taking such liberties with you, but I want you to know that I feared to look into your eyes because I knew I would find reflected there a merciless Indictment of my impotence and a compelling challenge to redeem my conquered manhood...what is the heart of all my black brothers for you and all your black sisters—and I fear I will fail unless you reach out to me, tune in on me with the antenna of your love, the sacred love in ultimate degree which you were unable to give me because, I being dead, was unworthy to receive it. (Cleaver, 1968, pp. 237–238)

Intra-racial love has at times been the source of adversity causing a rift between black men and black women. A separation of energies whereby black men and black women joust for positions concerning who has suffered more and whose suffering needs primary attention with respect to healing, restoration, and reclamation (Beale, 1970; Cleaver, 1968; Dyson, 2000). Cleaver was emotionally conflicted, battling his own self-hate and sexually criminal demons. A battle he suffered and lost when considering his treatment of black girls and women. However, this emotionally conflicted man managed to offer a selfish, side-stepping non-recognition of personal accountability, partly placing it on a failure of manhood that was primarily authored by white men. Cleaver then selfishly asks black women to somehow love him in a more unforgiving, unconditional manner. Moreover, Cleaver intimates that if this black woman refuses, then she perhaps will be the reason he will not engage in a loving relationship with her. As emotionally bankrupt and bizarre as it is, this is a begging proxy coming from Cleaver, that seems to resonate with black men, who called black women to action and sacrifice during social affirmation, civil rights, and social mobility movements starting in the 1930's and remaining in a post-modern society.

The love affair between black men and black women was contextualized by personhood affirmation movements, where charismatic black male leaders convinced black women to assume a supportive role in restoring black males as patriarchal powers at both the macro and micro levels. Intra-racial acceptance of Christian protocol and the social narrative of the Civil Rights movement seemed to install black men as figure heads, while relegating black women to second class citizenship. Black women agreed to be supportive but did not agree to the same type of physical and emotional domination, sexism and chauvinism that was comparable to colonialism.

The internal hurt is that black men betrayed black women by: (1) failing to deliver gender equity; (2) subjecting black women to sexual domination and abuse; (3) stifling, women's ambition; (4) being oppressive and intentionally silencing and/or being dismissive of feminist power brokerage; (5) infamously taking credit for liberation ideas, or in other words being intellectual currency pirates; (6) being racially disloyal by engaging in inter-racial relationships; (7) accusing black women of engaging in coalitions with white men to the demise of black men; and (8) blaming black women for losing patience and not remaining faithful to the idea that black male patriarchy would prove beneficial for black women, black families, and black communities. Essentially, black men manipulated black women under the umbrella of liberation, convincing black women that the struggle for freedoms would be successful when women assume a supportive role, and the rewards would be equitable. In other words, black men and black women would share in existential freedoms. Black women conceded only to be met with unfulfilled promises. Black men; therefore, owe black women because black women have loved black men enough to submit to them and sacrificed their personal ambitions (Cone, 1992; Dyson, 2000).

Accusing black women of being the black man's Achilles heel, leaving him in a condition worse than he was prior to interacting with her and accusing black women of engaging in racial coalitions with white men, to the demise of black men are accusations that have never been resolved.

Malcolm X states: I'd had too much experience that women were only tricky, deceitful, untrustworthy flesh. I had seen too many men ruined, or at least tied down, or in some other way messed up by women…How do you think this black man got in this state? By our women tricking him and tempting him and the devil taught her how to do this. The trickiest in existence is the black woman and the white man. If you go to court with your wife, she will always win over you because the devil can use her to break down more of our brothers…it is this evil black women in North America who does not want to do right and holds the man back from saving himself. (Cone, 1992, p. 275)

Malcolm X was rather vocal in blaming women for the conditions of black men. Dr. Martin Luther King Jr., believed in the intelligence of women but fell short in promoting such women to leadership positions in the movement. Both Malcolm X and Martin, seemed to be on the opposite ends of the spectrum with respect to the path towards human rights but did seem to find common ground relative to the need for black women to both submit to black men as head of household and best suited to lead progressive social movements. Apparently, these chauvinistic ideas leaked into their marriages and impacted the manner in which they spearheaded their respective movements (Cone, 1992). The resistance towards gender role equity in black nationalists and civil rights movements produced the Black Power Movement and fueled the resurgence of an unapologetic black feminist movement. It was obvious that black male freedom had become equivalent to black females not having freedom (Ture and Hamilton, 1992).

The trust that it necessary for black men and women to fully invest in a loving relationship remains fractured. It seems that many black men continue to blame black women for their life course conditions: (1) for trapping them into relationships; (2) for keeping them tied up in the court system; (3) for using children as bait and pawns for money; and (4) for prohibiting them from exercising freedoms to pursue happiness independent of black women. None of these charges have kept black men from having a double standard requiring black women to maintain exclusive relationships with them, while simultaneously continuing to be selfish and dismissive of black women's call for accountability.

Post-modern attempts at addressing the troubled tradition of black men and women loving one another has been an abysmal failure because black social narrative gatekeepers have anointed some black men as experts on relationships more than considering the merits of black feminism. When I tune into these so called male experts it is painfully apparent that they are operating without understanding the race legacy, social movement, and inequitable gender role contextual realities that are significantly related to intra-racial love. Black feminism represents a critical examination of race legacy, social movements, race and class intra-racial exploitation, co-optation and gender norm imposition. For this reason black feminism may not sound as appealing when compared to the surface level anecdotal offerings of a few males who have failed in relationships only to market themselves as relationship experts. There is a problem with romanticizing the failure of black men and blaming black women for those failures based on common negative stereotypes (Wanzo, 2011).

There is a desperate need for hard answers. There has to come a time when we stop anointing black men who have failed at relationships as relationship experts. These so called experts are "infatuation magicians" more than intellectual vessels versed in black feminist thought and/or disciplined by the intellectual capital derived from social affirmation movements.

> Dyson states: I became painfully aware, for the umpteenth time, of how messy, how maddeningly complex, are the relations between black men and black women. Why is it so difficult for brothers to hear the suffering of black women, to acknowledge their hurts, to embrace them as co-sufferers in a world where black skin and black bodies have been under extraordinary attack? Why is it so difficult for brothers to heal or at least help relieve, the bitter traumas of spirit and flesh that black women face, often at the end of a black man's hands or words? And why is it so difficult for sisters to see that because we live in a patriarchal society, black men represent a special challenge to white male power? …And yet, how can we reconcile intersection with specificity of pain? With the kind of pain that, yes, only black women can know. With the kind of pain that only black men can know. How can we make intersection and specificity work for us, use them as tools to uncover our common quest for humanity? (Dyson, 1996, pp. 199–200).

Dyson attempted to answer some of the questions through his speech *"Between Pain and Possibility"* during Minister Farrakhan's organized Million Man March in Washington D.C., in October of 1996. Dyson approaches answers by suggesting ways that black men can be saved by critical examination and self-disclosures specific to: (1) awareness that suffering has a vice grip on men; (2) acknowledging vulnerabilities and pain but not to the detriment of black women and children's pain; (3) understanding that cooperation not patriarchal rule is necessary for raising children; (4) dialing back machoism in an effort to cope with personal vulnerabilities;

(5) redefining masculinity as a willingness to embrace universal brotherhood beyond the perceived limits of sexual orientation; (6) burying the mantle of criminogenic pursuits and lethal predation as these are not manifestations of blacks' destiny; (7) surrendering tendencies to physically and emotionally abuse black women; and (8) engaging in creating coalitions aimed at

producing tangible opportunities for permanent underclass blacks to become full participants in the American Dream (Dyson, 1996, pp. 210–211).

This chapter was challenging because I am a black male and had honestly been temporarily entertained by black men's moral relativism on display through social and print journalism, and cultural outlets (music and movies). Now, I recognize that a critical analysis of intra-racial troubled relationships finds me far more concerned and embarrassed that there is a huge failure on the part of more than enough black men who continue to subject black women to inequitable power dynamics. Moreover, for cause that black men have reduced black women's vocal oppositions to disloyal chirping, or voices from the fringe of angry black women, I am again embarrassed. It's no wonder then that black love still remains a roller coaster of highs and lows.

> I agree with Dyson: Above all, it might just make us think about why too often black men and women who are in each other's beds are at each other's throats. And we don't have to fear that black women will see us as weak, or somehow conceding that we have been the sole source of conflict between the sexes all along. Millions of black women are still hungry for black men who don't mistake violence for strength, tenderness for weakness, or sensitivity for sentimentality (Dyson, 1996, pp. 205–206).

Black men, who have daughters are more likely to be concerned with how black love is being delivered to and received by black women. Black men with sons probably have reason to believe that the manner in which black men have traditionally loved black women is a status quo type of love and sufficient as long as their sons model their father's behavior. Lost in this approach to love are the voices of black women.

I have purposely focused on the troubling manner in which black men have loved black women from the 1930's through civil rights, social affirmation, and racial empowerment movements. The leaders of those movements were role models in their approach to securing human rights and were also points of reference for black masculine love. It was not so much that black women lost their voice or were silenced with respect to supporting and loving black men.

It was more about them sacrificing, having faith, delaying the gratification of gender equitability and believing black men's promises. I suspect black women were earnest in their hope and support for the redemption of black masculinity and actively participated in efforts to seize upon an empowering social status. Black women wanted black men to be respected and to have self-respect and believed that a return on their investment would be power dynamic reciprocation. Unfortunately, this kind of loving reciprocity did not manifest.

Black men can't continue to be naïve concerning how they have been loving and continue to love black women. Black men have a duty to engage in the type of masculinity that Du Bois, classified as the talented tenth. Meaning the intra-racial perils of the black community will be greatly improved by black men who have received proper upbringing and training specific to rescuing black people from oppressive conditions, inclusive of being agents of social healing for black women. Loving black women is the fundamental ingredient to intra-racial progress, family stability, and community healing. Perhaps, insulating black communities from inter-racial agents of destruction and violations to the black body is the obligations of the black man (Du Bois 1903). The most notable black leaders of the 60's, like Martin, Malcolm, and Huey voiced the reality that until black women have equitable progress, black men will remain in a troubled condition. Unfortunately, these men became receptive to this idea as their leadership tenure was progressively evolving but not soon enough because their respective leadership tenure was drawing to a close due to being murdered. There is no need to delay gender role equitability because it is the most important ingredient to a righteous kind of love from a black man to a black woman.

· 9 ·

CLOSURE IS ALL I NEED TO GET BY

Writing *The Social Construction of Black Masculinity: An Ethnographic Approach* was both challenging and at times cathartic because the content of this book is the result of balancing being a sociologists with emotional reflection, physical sacrifice and confronting a contested black manhood. When I think about the chapters of this book, it is hard to select a favorite. I remain attracted to the echoes of Du Bois, the timeliness of Dyson, West and Glaude. I appreciate my mentoring from Charles Tittle and give a huge nod of respect to the gangsters who I have come to know. I am a freshman of sorts when reading about black feminism and I have so much to learn. I've survived the violence of edge research and have been emotionally scarred by the classroom.

Chapter 1, *Scholarly Fingerprint: A Research Note*, provides my research production and was included in this book to familiarize readers with topics that are covered in African-American Criminology. My research, concentrates on the race variable so it represents a subfield of Criminology, which is a subfield of Sociology. My research at one point was mostly quantitative and did not deviate from examining well established theories on racial arrest differentials. Moreover, because racial outcomes are often collapsed into a class argument, my research examined a key component of social mobility, education. My scholarly goal was to make a contribution to the gang literature with respect to examining the legacy of black gangsterism as an early form of activism and then decoding the nuances of black gangsterism using an ethnographic approach.

Chapter 2, *I Will Dig a Ditch, Just Give Me My Good Name Back*, was cathartic, and allowed me to speak from outside the #MeToo movement. The other side of being falsely accused of sexual harassment. The students enrolled in the African-American Social Thought class, during the fall 2013 session witnessed a character assassination. Fall 2013, starting in September and lasting through the late spring 2014 semester represented the worst months of my academic profession. Although I was alone in that Title IX investigation, those students gave me the energy I needed to make it through. I honestly continue to feel they were rooting for me. We made it through together.

Chapter 3, *Du Bois' Souls of Black and White Folk: Can't Out Run Caste in America*, represented an early twentieth century examination of how blacks' humanity was regarded. The chapter included the perspectives, of Douglas, Crummell, Garvey, Malcolm X, Dyson, and Glaude in an effort to shed some insight about the equitability of blackness throughout the twentieth and early twenty first century. This chapter does not shy away from the fact that race remains a central component in social hierarchies with different consequences. Blacks' continue to suffer from negative consequences in instances where they reach too far in assuming that America is a post-racial society comprised of a universally accepted collective conscience that America is the land of respectable pluralism more than race related obstruction. Du Bois hammers the point that the oppressed are in the best position to not only understand their own oppression but to also describe the souls' of white folk. Du Bois' twentieth century perspectives present the black experience as the product of living behind a veil and having a double-consciousness.

Glaude's contention about the value gap is more evidence that there is racial inequity in the twenty first century. I hope this chapter will generate deep reflection and stimulate critical thought about race. I am only taking credit for being smart enough to re-introduce an examination of Du Bois' souls of black and white folk.

Chapter 4, *Policing Black Bodies: Lethal Predatory Habits* was a frustrating chapter because black bodies are slaughtered at the hands of police officers who appear to use the "fear for life" phrase in order to escape personal accountability, win a reasonable shooting decision, and maintain police officer integrity. Apparently, "fear" makes it reasonable to kill black males as young as twelve and as old as fifty. The black community only gets talking head, lip service that lacks sincerity from social control robots. Of course, I am tired of losing blacks to unnecessary lethal policing only to keep hearing about the tragedy of the event and of the learning experience that will result from another modern day lynching. I am tired of losing blacks to unnecessary lethal policing knowing family grief will be infinite. I am tired of losing blacks to unnecessary lethal policing and seeing the images replayed for public voyeurism. Blacks are being gunned down with visual clarity and left to bleed, much like a public hanging. The fascination with public lynching and disposable black corpses remains par for the course for white America. Public display of black corpses has again surfaced to become on demand, episode viewing material for black America. I am tired of losing blacks to unnecessary lethal policing and witnessing the tears, hearing the sounds of one-sided mourning, and digesting the constant losing in the court room. In any sport, if you lose more than you win, then you are considered a loser so it is in that light that legal counsel, lawyers, prosecutors and grand jury participants are considered losers. Ironically, the only winner is the police officer.

Prayers and condolences are heartless until prayers stop the need for condolences. Pray for the change of heart regarding the veil that black people experience. Pray for the infusion of humanity that delivers reverence of life for those carrying instruments of death. Pray for legal agents because they are woefully inadequate at delivering justice. Pray for the collective conscience, particularly the kind that claim spirituality. Spirituality and inhumanity can't reside in the same body, unless that spirituality be fake. Perhaps there is a version of spirituality that positions the Holy Trinity as white and; therefore, jurisdictional with a partial loan to the black body. In other words, the unresolved nature of black inhumanity is due to the fundamental premise that God is white, the covenant covers only whites and blackness in similar fashion to darkness represents the enemy and; therefore, is not desired.

Chapter 5, *Protest Spirit: Bastardized Activism in Gangsterism*, positioned black gangsterism as potentially civil, criminogenic, healthy and unhealthy for black communities. This chapter is not intended to promote black gangsterism as noble but to reposition black gangs as socially constructed by racial conflict and then progressing towards full engagement in deviance, crime, violence and lethal predation. Farrakhan has traditionally been hard on black communities regardless of class. Farrakhan promotes racial independence, functional patriarchal rule, disciplined black manhood, personal accountability, and responsibility for the social ills occurring in black communities.

Farrakhan states: Look at my people. Drive-by shootings. Carjackings. Is that the work of a righteous people? That's the work of the devil. We have fallen short of the glory of God. My people are not dying from skinheads. They're not dying from the Ku Klux Klan. They're dying from their ignorance and self-hatred that has us destroying one another. We can't blame Jews. We can't blame Koreans or Vietnamese who take money out of our community. ..We have to blame ourselves, because we've been offered the chance to go to the best schools to get an education, but we have not come out and used that education to provide the goods and education that our own communities need (Magida, 1996, p. 140).

Farrakhan's remarks are similar to Du Bois' talented tenth perspective. In this chapter, I call for a youth liberation movement that is contingent upon gangsters engaging in a cease fire, preserving life, instead of participating in killing campaigns. Decreasing black-on-black victimization will minimize the unspoken fears that non-resident blacks have, and perhaps open up communication leading to progressive coalitions that will improve permanent underclass communities.

Chapter 6, *Edge Research: Taking in Ganglands and Violent Scenes*, presented a cautionary tale about engaging in ethnographic research long term. The notes were B-side, which means the content was at times obscene, pornographic, racially insensitive, sexist, and lacked political correctness. Chapter six, did omit observations from Latino night and the nuances of negotiating peace when rival black gangs end up in the same club. Typically, Latino night was reserved for security training. The inside commentary was that Mexicans fight hard and are at times unstoppable so new security were required to work in order to test their mantle. My observations from working on these nights are: (1) Latinos are quick to call black people, nigga; (2) the presence of MS13 and members of the Almighty Latin King Nation in the same club is a recipe for violence; (3) it was important to have Spanish speaking personnel; (4) Pun, our resident Puerto Rican, Rolling 60's Crip was a Godsend because he held rapport with gang members; (5) whistling throughout the club is a warning for potential violence and/or that a brawl is underway; (6) stay clear of domestic altercations or at least get someone who is with the combating party to intercede, unless you want to end up getting jumped for trying to break up a fight; (7) the domestic violence was oftentimes initiated by females but once males lost self-control, the beatings were brutal; and (8) no matter the intensity of violence, police officers were never called and in fact, club patrons requested that the police not be called.

Greensboro, North Carolina is a Blood gang city or at least it seemed to be dominated by Greensboro's South Side collection of neighborhoods that affiliated with Bloods. There also seemed to be tension between Greensboro's Bloods and the Bloods that came from Raleigh/Durham, North Carolina. The source of the tension was never really made clear but what seemed apparent was that Bloods from the Raleigh/Durham area thought they were representing the violent "Be Bloody Code" more than the Bloods from Greensboro. In order to maintain peace, security sided with the patrons we knew more than new faces. In other words, security formed an uneasy alliance with the local gangs that frequented the clubs and usually reserved specific areas in the club just for their crew. Moreover, complimentary drinks were sent to the leaders as a way to maintain positive communication and diplomacy. It is far better to allow the gang leaders to police their own as opposed to security stepping in because then security becomes gang like. Clashes between security and gang members never end well and controlling violence fades into the background as aggressive masculinity takes priority. It becomes more about individual respect, social status and street justice. A group of individual security guards can easily become gang like and even consider themselves comrades, which is forged through experiencing violence.

Chapter 7, *Hulking Out: White Males Response to Bullying, Humiliation, Rejection, Intimidation and Perceived Injustice in an Academic Setting,* examined mass shootings. The evidence reveals: (1) mass shootings are more than likely the result of strategic planning and less likely to be due to mental health issues; (2) mass shootings are more likely committed by white males than black males; (3) white males are more likely to engage in mass and/or rampage shootings on school grounds because of differing experiences with white privilege; and (4) black males are more likely to engage in target shooting given they subscribe to street codes.

Part of dealing with the mass shooting equation is to consistently recognize that white males are disproportionately involved. What's more there should be less energy given to storylines that elevate the character of the mass shooter because it becomes an indirect excuse for mass shootings. Certainly, rushing to conclude that mental health is the number one reason, while helping to defuse a moral panic does decline from expressing the probability that white males are strategically planning to murder in mass. This chapter was not intended to be racial more than it was intended to suggest that violence has often been the result of socialization except it continues to be covered as if violence is the product of blacks' criminality.

Chapter 8, *A Love of Our Own: The Manner in Which Black Men Love,* examined the troublesome blueprint millions of black men have been using to love black women. The manner in which black men have loved black women has been dominated by the assumption that black men need to be restored and empowered, while women assume the supportive role has morphed into black women being exploited by black men. Mutual accusations of betrayal and arguing about suffering has negatively impacted intra-racial relationships. Cleaver's apocalyptic fusion and the content of his love letter to black women were included in this chapter. Cleaver is controversial and for many he represents a reprehensible, abomination for raping black girls as practice for raping white women. Why even include him when it is obvious his rapist's mentality is ill conceived, morally bankrupt and depraved on every level?

> Huey states: He practiced on black women in order to acquire perfection for his rape of white women. This implies not only envy of the female principle but contempt for blackness, combining the elements of self-hatred and repressed sexual needs. Cleaver degrades black women twice, first by rape and second by viewing it as a dress rehearsal. By practicing on blacks he expresses his admiration for whites. He in fact pays white women a childish compliment: He ascends the heights to their vaginas by stepping on the bodies of black women! (Hilliard and Weise, 2002, pp. 288–289).

Cleaver suggested that he was born again. Reborn into a newness of loving blackness and black women, and that this born again disposition should excuse his rapist's mode of operation. He contends that the forgiving nature and love of black women would complete his return, his fusion with the black women he claims to love. Therefore, Chapter 8 includes Cleaver for reason of provocation, critical thinking, and perhaps even the discovery of the irony about black love that comes from a bottom of the barrel human being. Moreover, is Cleaver's offering more precise than the Hill Harper, Steve Harvey, Tyler Perry, Tim Alexander and the T. D. Jakes' types, out there peddling some version of interplay between secular and spiritually dominant and fractured masculinity?

What's left? I have emptied my reservoir for each chapter in this book. The completion of this book means I have climbed the last mountain. Only time that I may or may not have will determine what is next and if there is nothing more required of me then this book will have to be finally enough.

REFERENCES

Alexander, M. (2010). *The New Jim Crow: Mass Incarceration in the Age of Colorblindness*. New York: New Press.

Alonso, A. (1999). Territoriality Among African-American Street Gang in Los Angeles. Un-published Master's Thesis.

Anderson, E. (1999). *Code of the Street*. New York: W.W. Norton.

Anderson, E. (1990). *Street Wise*. Chicago: The University Press of Chicago.

Andriolo, K. (1998). Gender and the Cultural Construction of Good and Bad Suicides. *Suicide and Life-Threatening Behavior*, 28(1): 37–49.

Agnew, R. (2006). *Pressured into Crime: An Overview of General Strain Theory*. Oxford: Oxford University Press.

Agnew, R. (2005). *Why Do Criminals Offend?: A General Theory of Crime and Delinquency*. Los Angeles, CA: Roxbury Publishing.

Arlington County (VA). (1999). Statement on racial Profiling. Subject to Debate. December's Washington, DC Police Executive Research Forum.

Beale, F. (1970). Double Jeopardy: To Be Black and Female. In T. C. Bambara (ed.), *The Black Woman: An Anthology* (pp. 108–122). New York: Washington Square Press.

Becker, H. (1963). *Outsiders: Studies in the Sociology of Deviance*. New York: Basic Books.

Boustan, L. (2015). The Great Black Migration: Opportunity and Competition in Northern Labor Markets. *Focus*, 32(1): 24–26.

Boyd, T. (1997). *Am I Black Enough for You? Popular Culture from the Hood and Beyond*. Indiana: Indiana University Press.

Breitman, G. (1965). *Malcolm X Speaks: Selected Speeches and Statements*. New York: Grove Weidenfeld.

Broome, H. (1979). Forward. In R. N. Brenner and M. Kravitz (compilation editors), *A Community Concern: Police use of Deadly Force*. Washington, DC: United States Department of Justice, National Institute of Law Enforcement and Criminal Justice.

Brotz, H. (1966). *Negro Social and Political Thought 1850–1920: Representative Texts*. New York: Basic Books.

Canetto, S. (1997). Meanings of Gender and Suicidal Behavior in Adolescence. *Suicide and Life Threatening Behavior*, 27(4): 339–351.

Cannon, K. (2004). Slave Ideology and Biblical Interpretations. In J. Bobo, C. Hudley, and C. Michel (eds.), *The Black Studies Reader* (pp. 413–420). New York: Routledge.

Carlson, D. (2005). *When Cultures Clash: Strategies for Strengthened Police-Community Relations*. (2nd Edition). New Jersey: Pearson Prentice Hall.

Casella, R. (2001). *Being Down: Challenging Violence in Urban Schools*. New York: Teachers College Press.

Chatterton, W. (2010). *Losing My Cool: Love Literature and a Black Man's Escape from the Crowd*. New York: Penguin Press.

Cleaver, E. (1968). *Soul on Ice*. New York: Random House.

Cohen, A. (1955). *Delinquent Boys: The Culture of the Gang*. New York: Free Press.

Collins, A. (2019). The Media Assault on the Black Male: Echoes of Public Lynching and Killing the Modern Terror of Jack Johnson. In T. S. Ransaw, C. P. Gause, and R. Majors (eds.), *Handbook of Research on Black Males* (pp. 507–516). Michigan: Michigan State Press.

Collins, P. (2004). *Black Sexual Politics: African-Americans, Gender, And the New Racism*. New York: Routledge, Taylor & Francis Group.

Cone, J. (1992). *Martin & Malcolm & America: A Dream or a Nightmare*. New York: Orbis Books.

Cornish, D., and Clarke, R. (1986). *The Reasoning Criminal: Rational Choice Perspectives on Offending*. New York: Springer-Verlag.

Cureton, S. (2019a). Introduction. In T. S. Ransaw, C. P. Gause, and R. Majors (eds.), *Handbook of Research on Black Males* (pp. 467–470). Michigan: Michigan State Press.

Cureton, S. (2019b). Hoovers and Night Crawlers: When Outside In Becomes Inside Out. In T. S. Ransaw, C. P. Gause, and R. Majors (eds.), *Handbook of Research on Black Males* (pp. 531–548), Michigan: Michigan State Press.

Cureton, S. (2017). CHIRAQ: Oppression, Homicide, Concentrated Misery, and Gangsterism in Chicago. *Journal of Gang Research*, 22(1): 1–18.

Cureton, S., and Wilson C. (2012). The Deceptive Black Knight Campaign: Clique Loyalty and Sexual Conquest. *Journal of Black Masculinity*, 2(3): 1–24.

Cureton, S. (2011). *Black Vanguards and Black Gangsters: From Seeds of Discontent to a Declaration of War*. Maryland: University Press of America.

Cureton, S. (2011). Night-Crawlers: The Potential Health Risks Associated with Criminogenic Masculinity and Clubbing. *Journal of Black Masculinity*, 2(1): 135–151.

Cureton, S. (2010). Lost Souls of Society Become Hypnotized by Gangsterism. *Journal of Gang Research*, 18(1): 39–52.

Cureton, S. (2009). Something Wicked This Way Comes: A Historical Account of Black Gangsterism Offers Wisdom and Warning for African-American Leadership. *Journal of Black Studies*, 40(2): 347–361.

Cureton, S. (2008). *Hoover Crips: When Cripin' Becomes a Way of Life*. Maryland: University Press of America.

Cureton, S., and Bellamy, R. (2007, Spring/Winter). Gangster "Blood" Over College Aspirations: The Implications of Gang Membership for One Black Male College Student. *Journal of Gang Research*, 14(2): 31–39.

Cureton, S. (2003). Race-Specific College Student Experiences on a Predominantly White Campus. *The Journal of Black Studies*, 33(3): 295–311.

Cureton, S. (2002). Introducing Hoover: I'll Ride for You Gangsta. In C. R. Huffs (ed.), *Gangs in America III*. Thousand Oaks: Sage.

Cureton, S. (2002). An Assessment of Wilson and Frazier's Perspectives on Race and Racial Life Chances. *African-American Research Perspectives*, 8(1): 47–54.

Cureton, S. (2001). An Empirical Test of the Social Threat Phenomenon: Using 1990 Census and Uniform Crime Reports. *Journal of Criminal Justice*, 29(2): 157–166.

Cureton, S. (2000). Justifiable Arrests or Discretionary Justice: Predictors of Racial Arrest Differentials. *Journal of Black Studies*, 30(5): 703–719.

Cureton, S. (2000). Determinants of Black/White Arrest Differential: A Review of the Literature. In M. W. Markowitz and D. John-Brown's (eds.), *The System in Black and White: Exploring the Connections Between Race, Crime and Justice* (pp. 65–72). Connecticut: Praeger Publishers.

Cureton, S. (1999). Differential Black/White Arrest Rates: Offending Behavior or Discretionary Justice. *African-American Research Perspectives*, 5(1): 74–80.

Davis, S., and Block, A. (2018). A Critical Analysis of the Shootings of Unarmed African Americans by Police: A Social Work Perspective. *Keystone Journal of Undergraduate Research*, 5(1): 1–11.

Dawley, D. (1992). *A Nation of Lords*. Illinois: Waveland Press.

Daynes, S., and Williams, T. (2018). *On Ethnography*. Massachusetts: Polity Press.

Dennis, K. (2019). Black male suicide: Inward expressed frustration and aggression. In T. S. Ransaw, C. P. Gause, and R. Majors (eds.), *Handbook of Research on Black Males* (pp. 489–505). Michigan: Michigan State Press.

Dikel, W. (2012). School Shootings and Student Mental Health-What Lies Beneath the Tip of the Iceberg. *NSBA Council of School Attorneys*. Reprinted with permission.

Dobbin, F. (1993). The Social Construction of the Great Depression: Industrial Policy During the 1930's in the United States, Britain, and France. *Theory and Society*, 22(1): 1–56.

Du Bois, W. E. B. [1904](1978). The Relations of the Negroes to the Whites in the South. In D. S. Green and E. D. Driver (eds.), *Du Bois' On Sociology and the Black Community* (pp. 253–270). Chicago: University of Chicago Press.

Du Bois, W. E. B. (1953). *Souls of Black Folk: Essays and Sketches*. Connecticut: Fawcett Publications.

Du Bois, W. E. B. (1920). The Souls of White Folk. In *Darkwater, Visions from Within the Veil* (pp. 453–465). New York: Harcourt and Brace.

Du Bois, W. E. B. (1903). *The Talented Tenth*. An Essay by W.E.B. Du Bois.

Dyson, M. E. (2000). *I May Not Get There With You: The True Martin Luther King. Jr*. New York: The Free Press.

Dyson, M. E. (1996). *Race Rules: Navigating the Color Line*. New York: Vintage Books.

Eberhardt, J., Purdie, V., Goff, P., and Davies, P. (2004). Seeing Black: Race, Crime, and Visual Processing. *Journal of Personality and Social Psychology*, 87(6): 876–893.

Estes, S. (2005). *I Am a Man: Race Manhood and the Civil Rights Movement*. North Carolina: University of North Carolina Press.

Fantz, A., Knight, L., and Wang, K. (2014). How Many School Shootings Since Newton? *CNN Latest News*.

Fast, J. (2008). *Ceremonial Violence: A Psychological Explanation of School Shootings*. New York: The Overlook Press.

Feldman, H., and Aldrich, M. (2005). The Role of Ethnography in Substance Abuse Research and Public Policy. In *Cocktails and Dreams: Perspectives on Drug and Alcohol Use* (pp. 14–28). New Jersey: Pearson Prentice Hall.

Felson, R., Allen, L., South, S., and McNulty, T. (1994). The Subculture of Violence: Individual vs. School Context Effects. *Social Forces*, 73(1): 155–173.

Fessenden, F. (2000). They Threaten Seethe and Unhinge, Then Kill in Quantity. *New York Times*.

Finkelstein, M. (2005). *With No Direction: Homeless Youth on the Road and in the Streets*. California: Thomson Wadsworth.

Flacks, R., and Turkel, G. (1978). Radical Sociology: The Emergence of Neo-Marxian Perspectives in US Sociology. *Annual Review of Sociology*, 4: 193–238.

Foner, P. (1970). *The Black Panthers Speak*. New York: Da Capo Press.

Fox, J., and Burstein, H. (2010). *Violence and Security on Campus: From Preschool to College*. California: Praeger.

Fox, J., Levin, J., and Quinet, K. (2005). *The Will to Kill: Making Sense of Senseless Murder*. Second Edition. New York: Pearson.

Frazier, F. (1968). *Race Relations*. Chicago: The University of Chicago Press.

Garrow, D. (1953). *The FBI and Martin Luther King, Jr*. New York: Penguin Books.

Gilbert, K., and Ray, R. (2016). Why Police Kill Black Males with Impunity: Applying Public Health Critical Race Praxis (PHCRP) to Address the Determinants of Policing Behaviors and "Justifiable" Homicides in the USA. *Journal of Urban Health: Bulletin of the New York Academy of Medicine*, 93(1): 122–140.

Gilligan, J. (1997). *Violence*. New York: Vintage Books.

Glaude, E. (2016). *Democracy in Black How Race Still Enslaves The American Soul*. New York: Crown Publishers.

Gray, H. (1995). Black Masculinity and Visual Culture. *Callaloo*, 18(2): 401–405.

Haley, A. (1964). *The Autobiography of Malcolm X*. New York: Ballantine Books.

Hagedorn, J. (2009). A Genealogy of Gangs in Chicago: Brining the State Back into Gang Research. *Global Gangs: Comparative Perspective*. University of Illinois Press. Chapter initially presented at Global Gangs Conference, Geneva Switzerland.

Hagedorn, J. (2006). Race not Space: A Revisionist History of Gangs in Chicago. *The Journal of American History*, 91(2): 194–208.

Hall, R. (2009). Cool Pose, Black Manhood and Juvenile Delinquency. *Journal of Human Behavior in the Social Environment*, 19(5): 531–539.

Harro, B. (2000). The Cycle of Socialization. In M. Adams, W. J. Blumenfeld, R. Castaneda, H. W. Hackman, M. L. Peters, and X. Zuniga (eds.), *Readings for Diversity and Social Justice* (pp. 337–339). New York: Routledge.

Hempel, A., Meloy, J., and Richards, C. (1999). Offenders and Offense Characteristics of a Non-random Sample of Mass Murderers. *Journal of the American Academy of Psychiatry and Law*, 27: 213–225.

Hernandez, K-Ann. (2014). Advancing Research on Religious/Spiritual Affiliation and Construction of Black Masculinity. In C. Gause (ed.), *Black Masculinity in America: Can I get a Witness?* (pp. 9–33). Florida: Book Locker.

Hilliard, D., Zimmerman, K., and Zimmerman, K. (2006). *Huey: Spirit of the Panther*. New York: Thunder's Mouth Press.

Hilliard, D., and Weise, D. (2002). *The Huey P. Newton Reader*. New York: Seven Stories Press.

Hooley, J., and Gotlib, I. (2000). A Diathesis-Stress Conceptualization of Expressed Emotion and Clinical Outcome. *Applied and Preventive Psychology*, 9: 135–151.

Kalish, R., and Kimmel, M. (2010). Suicide by Mass Murder: Masculinity, Aggrieved Entitlement, and Rampage School Shootings. *Health Sociology Review*, 19(4): 451–464.

Katz, J. (1988). *Seductions of Crime: Moral and Sensual Attractions to Doing Evil*. New York: Basic Books.

Kazuhisa, H. (2009). Postwar Civil Rights Politics in the United States: Understanding the Dynamics of Democratization from a Global Perspective. *Nanzan Review of American Studies*, 31: 179–193.

Kimmel, M. (2008). Profiling School Shooters and Shooters' Schools: The Cultural Contexts of Aggrieved Entitlement and Restorative Masculinity. In B. Agger and T. W. Luke (eds.), *There is a Gunman on Campus: Terror at Virginia Tech* (pp. 65–78). Maryland: Rowman and Littlefield.

Kimmel, M., and Mahler, M. (2003). Adolescent Masculinity, Homophobia and Violence: Random School Shootings, 1982–2001. *American Behavioral Scientist*, 46(10): 1439–1458.

Klein, J. (2012). *The Bully Society: School Shootings and the Crisis of Bullying in America's Schools*. New York: New York University Press.

Ladson-Billings, G. (1995). But That's Just Good Teaching! The Case for Culturally Relevant Pedagogy. *Theory into Practice*, 34(3): 159–165.

Langman, P. (2009). *Why Kids Kill: Inside the Minds of School Shooters*. New York: Palgrave MacMillan.

Larkin, R. (2007). *Comprehending Columbine*. Pennsylvania: Temple University Press.

Leary, M., Kowalski, R., Smith, L., and Phillips S. (2003). Teasing Rejection and Violence: Case Studies of the School Shootings. *Aggressive Behavior*, 29(3): 202–214.

Levin, J., and Fox, J. (2001). *Deadlines: Essays in Murder and Mayhem.* Boston: Allyn and Bacon.

Love, B., and Tosolt, B. (2014). African Americans' Double Consciousness after the Election of Barack Obama: "This is America After All." In C. Gause (ed.), *Black Masculinity in America: Can I get a Witness?* (pp. 181–203). Florida: Book Locker.

Magida, A. (1996). *The Prophet of Rage: A Life of Louis Farrakhan and His Nation.* New York: Basic Books.

Mastro, D., Lapinski, M., Kopacz, M., and Behm-Morawitz, E. (2009). The Influence of Exposure to Depictions of Race and Crime in TV News on Viewer's Social Judgments. *Journal of Broadcasting and Electronic Media*, 53(4): 615–635.

Majors, R. (1993). *Cool Pose: The Dilemmas of Black Manhood in America.* New York: Simon & Schuster.

Majors, R. and Billson, J. (1992). *Cool Pose.* New York: Lexington Books.

Meloy, J., Hempel, A., Mohandie, K., Shiva, A., and Gray, T. (2001). Offender and offense characteristics of a nonrandom sample of adolescent mass murderers. *Journal of the American Academy of Child and Adolescent Psychiatry*, 40: 719–728.

McCall, N. (1994). *Makes Me Wanna Holler: A Young Black Man in America.* New York: Vintage Books.

McGee, J., and DeBernardo, C. (1999). The Classroom Avenger. *The Forensic Examiner*, 8(5–6): 16–18.

Monell, J. (2019). A Preliminary Examination of Hegemonic Masculinity: Definitional Transference of Black Masculinity Effecting Lethal Tactics against Black Males. In T. S. Ransaw, C. P. Gause, and R. Majors (eds.), *Handbook of Research on Black Males* (pp. 517–530). Michigan: Michigan State Press.

Muschert, G. (2007). Research in School Shootings. *Sociology Compass*, 1(1): 60–80.

Neely, C. (2015). *You're Dead So What? Media, Police, and the Invisibility of Black Women as Victims of Homicide.* Michigan: Michigan State University Press.

Newman, K., Fox, C., Roth, W., Mehta, J., and Harding, D. (2004). *Rampage: The Social Roots of School Shootings.* New York: Basic Books.

Nirvi, S., and Maxwell, L. (2012). Researchers Sound Alarm over Black Student Suspensions. *EdWeek.org.*

Ocejo, R. (2013). *Ethnography and the City: Readings on Doing Urban Field Work.* New York: Routledge.

Oliver, W. (1989). Black Males and Social Problems: Prevention Through Afrocentric Socialization. *Journal of Black Studies*, 20(1): 15–39.

Preti, A. (2006). Suicide to Harass Others: Clues from Mythology to Understanding Suicide Bombing Attacks. *The Journal of Crisis Intervention and Suicide Prevention*, 27(1): 22–30.

Range, L., and Leach, M. (1998). Gender Culture and Suicidal Behavior: A Feminist Critique of Theories and Research. *Suicide and Life-Threatening Behavior*, 28(1): 24–36.

Rankine, C. (2016). The Condition of Black Life Is One of Mourning. In C. Williams, K. E. Williams, and K. N. Blain (eds.), *Charleston Syllabus: Readings on Race, Racism, and Racial Violence* (pp. 71–77). Georgia: University of Georgia Press.

Raper, A. (1933). *The Tragedy of Lynching*. Chapel Hill: The University of North Carolina Press.

Reddy, M., Borum, R., Berglund, J., Vossekuil, B., Fein, R., and Modzeleski, W. (2001). Evaluating Risk for Targeted Violence in Schools: Comparing Risk Assessment, Threat Assessment, and Other Approaches. *Psychology in the Schools*, 38(2): 157–172.

Rocque, M. (2012). Exploring School Rampage Shootings: Research, Theory and Policy. *The Social Science Journal*, 49(3): 304–313.

Rothenberg, P. (2002). *White Privilege: Essential Readings on the Other Side of Racism*. New York: Worth Publishing.

Sawyer, E. (1973). Methodological Problems in Studying So-Called "Deviant" Communities. In J. A. Ladner's (ed.), *The Death of White Sociology* (pp. 361–379). New York: Vintage Books.

Schwyzer, H. (2012). *Why Most Mass Murderers Are Privileged White Men*. Role Reboot.

Shakur, S. (1993). *Monster: The Autobiography of an L. A. Gang Member*. New York: Penguin Press.

Simpkins, L. (2019). Victimized VICTIM: The Consciousness of Black Femininity in the Image of Masculinity. In T. S. Ransaw, C. P. Gause, and R. Majors (eds.), *Handbook of Research on Black Males* (pp. 471–487). Michigan: Michigan State Press.

Stack, S., and Wasserman, I. (2009). Gender and Suicide Risk: The Role of Wound Site. *Suicide and Life-Threatening Behavior*, 39(1): 13–20.

Sullivan, M., and Guerette, R. (2003). The Copycat Factor: Mental Illness, Guns and The Shooting Incident at Heritage High School, Rockdale County Georgia. In M. H. Moore, C. V. Petrie, A. A. Braga, and B. L. McLaughlin (eds.), *Deadly Lesson: Understanding Lethal School Violence* (pp. 25–69). Washington DC: NAP.

Terry, W. (2006). *Bloods: Black Veterans of the Vietnam War: An Oral History*. New York: Ballantine Books.

Thrasher, F. (1927). *The Gang*. Chicago: University of Chicago Press.

Tucker, S. (1968). *Beyond the Burning: Life and Death of the Ghetto*. New York: Association Press.

Tuck, M., and David, R. (1986). The Theory of Reasoned Action: A Decision Theory of Crime. In D. Cornish and R. V. Clarke (eds.), *The Reasoning Criminal: Rational Choice Perspectives on Offending* (pp. 156–169). New York: Springer-Verlag.

Ture, K., and Hamilton, C. (1992). *Black Power: The Politics of Liberation*. New York: Vintage Books

Vossekuil, B., Fein, R., Reddy, M., Borum, R., and Modzeski, W. (2002). *The Final report and Findings of the Safe School Initiative: Implications for the Prevention of School Attacks in the United States*. Washington DC: U.S. Department of Education, Office of Elementary and Secondary, Safe and Drug-Free Schools Program and U.S. Secret Service, National Threat Assessment Center.

Wallace, D. (2007). It's a M-A-N Thang: Black Male Gender Role Socialization and the Performance of Masculinity in Love Relationships. *Journal of Pan African Studies*, 1(7): 11–22.

Wanzo, R. (2001). Black Love is Not a Fairytale, Sexing the Colorlines: Black Sexualities, Popular Culture, and Cultural Production. *Poroi*, 7(2): 1–18.

Washington, H. (2006). *Medical Apartheid: The Dark History of Medical Experimentation on Black Americans from Colonial Times to the Present*. New York: Harlem Moon.

Webster, M., and Rashotte, L. (2009). Fixed Roles and Situated Actions. *Sex Roles*, 61: 325–337.

Welch, K. (2007). Black Criminal Stereotypes and Racial Profiling. *Journal of Contemporary Criminal Justice*, 23: 276–288.

West, C. (2001). *Race Matters*. New York: Vintage Books.

Wilkerson, I. (2010). *The Warmth of Other Suns: The Epic Story of America's Great Migration*. New York: Random House.

Williams, S. (2004). *Blue Rage Black Redemption*. California: Damamli Publishing.

Wilson, W. (2009). *More Than Just Race: Being Black and Poor in the Inner City*. New York: W. W. Norton.

Wilson, W. (1996). *When Work Disappears: The World of the New Urban Poor*. New York Knopf.

Wilson, W. (1987). *The Truly Disadvantaged: The Inner City, The Underclass, and Public Policy*. Chicago: University of Chicago Press.

Wright II, E., and Calhoun, T. (2006). Jim Crow Sociology: Toward an Understanding of the Origin and Principles of Black Sociology via The Atlanta Sociological Laboratory. *Sociological Focus*, 39(1): 1–18.

INDEX

E

F

G

H